WHAT PEOPLE

ENSO

This simple and profound book, written from the depths of the soul, will touch your soul and awaken it to joy and courage and peace.
Andrew Harvey, author of *The Direct Path: Creating a Personal Journey to the Divine Using the World's Spiritual Traditions*

Whenever I sit to read one of Jacob's daily meditations, and I do so several days each week, a sense of calm flows through me. I become quiet, my thoughts settle down, and I remember who I am and what is important. I am grateful for this gift.
Nancy Reuben, MD

I find that reading Morning Blessing Letters allows me to transition into each day feeling centered in myself and grounded in the moment. Each letter directs me to practices I can return to during the day. I enjoy selecting a letter at random and seeing what in it speaks to me

that day.
Frederick Gates, PhD, clinical psychologist

Reading Morning Blessing Letters each morning gets me started on the day in a more conscious and centered state of mind, putting me in touch with the blessings of life and the essential tools I have to draw on.
Rev. Joel Grossman, interfaith minister

This beautiful book of Morning Blessing Letters is a source of comfort and inspiration for me.
Miriam Greenspan, author of *Healing Through the Dark Emotions*

Enso Morning

Daily Meditation Gifts

Enso Morning

Daily Meditation Gifts

Jacob Watson

BOOKS

Winchester, UK
Washington, USA

First published by O-Books, 2016
O-Books is an imprint of John Hunt Publishing Ltd., Laurel House, Station Approach,
Alresford, Hants, SO24 9JH, UK
office1@jhpbooks.net
www.johnhuntpublishing.com

For distributor details and how to order please visit the 'Ordering' section on our website.

ISBN: 978 1 78535 298 0
Library of Congress Control Number: 2015950498

A CIP catalogue record for this book is available from the British Library.

Design: Lee Nash

Printed and bound by CPI Group (UK) Ltd, Croydon, CR0 4YY, UK

CONTENTS

Also by Jacob Watson:

Essence: The Emotional Path to Spirit

To Kristine

Introduction

The Morning Blessing Letters in *Enso Morning* were written first as my own morning meditation. For over six months of weekdays I would get up early in the morning and meditate, sometimes after a walk outside, building on over thirty-five years of morning sitting meditation. A rhythm had evolved over the years whereby I would first tune in to the fact that I was alive and felt welcomed by the spirit of the new day, something larger than myself that was not only aware of my existence sitting there on the cushion, but indeed glad to have me sitting there and present for the opening of the day together. This extraordinary bonding – sometimes against all odds because I felt lonely or insignificant or useless – grounded me in the present moment. A natural next step was to do… nothing. But to stay precisely there in the moment that had become still and sacred. Silence naturally ensued. I felt encouraged to just stay there in the stillness, so I did. The silence became a blessing, then a gift came.

Morning Blessing Letters became my thesis to

complete the Doctor of Ministry program at Matthew Fox's University of Creation Spirituality. As soon as I finished a Morning Blessing Letter in the morning, I e-mailed it to a list of colleagues and friends. Every letter was written in a carefully designed form to wake up, encourage and support health-care workers and chaplains in their daily work with patients and caregivers. I also distributed them by hand to hospitals and agencies, and to counselors and other individuals in care-giving settings. I enjoyed walking up to the nurses' stations at Maine Medical Center, where staff members were surrounded by white paper – in the midst of their urgent responsibilities – and leaving them a Morning Blessing Letter printed on pink paper. I delighted in slipping a Morning Blessing Letter under the door at an agency or dropping one off at a friend's counseling office to offer as a surprise gift with which to begin their morning.

In more concise terms, each Morning Blessing Letter in *Enso Morning* has seven focusing paragraphs:

1 Welcome

2 Silent meditation

3 Affirmation of physical self

4 Affirmation of emotional self

5 Affirmation of spiritual self

6 Blessing for the day

7 Gift for the day

Intention for Use

It is my hope that you read the Morning Blessing Letters in *Enso Morning* to stimulate and deepen your own spiritual and meditation practice. I encourage you to use each paragraph to center yourself in the morning, to give loving attention to each part of yourself as an intentional and practical way to nurture your whole being at the beginning of the day.

Open the book at random and trust that the appropriate and meaningful letter will appear in your hands. Or, when you have a specific longing or particular need, use the Table of Contents to consciously select the Gift named on the left side of the page, and open to that letter indicated by the page number on the right side of the page.

Occasionally a letter might seem 'off', as if it were not meant for you. You may not live in New England, and experience the marked differences in spring, summer, fall and winter. The season, the topic, the place, the setting – even the gift – might seem foreign or irrelevant. Yet we all have 'seasons of the soul'. This is the time to recall that what is perceived as 'outer' also can be true inside, that perceived separation is but an illusion, and that *everything* is a metaphor, that is, it refers to something real inside your being, for you are indeed one with all.

Sometimes you may find that a specific gift is just what you wanted or imagined and hoped for and, lo and behold, here it is. Other times you may be puzzled, and not understand your particular gift. Remember, many of life's gifts are unbidden, unseen, unexpected, only to unfold their richness and meaning with time.

The Morning Blessing Letters in *Enso Morning* center, support and awaken readers to begin their day awakened and encouraged to be themselves, joined with like-minded souls. I encourage you to share these letters with friends, family and colleagues.

The three concluding letters give gifts inspired by the ancient mantra Sat, Chit, Ananda. These Sanskrit words can be translated Existence, Consciousness, Bliss. Used in daily morning meditation, these precious words offer us energetic encouragement to abide in the essence of life. Blended together, these words form Saccidananda, the name of the Hindu-Christian Ashram in South India where Bede Griffiths lived and taught. In 2015 I made a month-long pilgrimage to Saccidananda – also called Shantivanam – for meditation and prayer. I use Sat, Chit, Ananda as a mantra for my daily meditations, both in India and back at home, wherever I am.

Zen Enso Circles

The Enso circles that decorate this book are an ancient art form blending art and religion. While these circles are thought of as Buddhist, in fact they have origins in several wisdom traditions, including Hindu, Buddhist and Taoist, making them interfaith in character. For example, in the Hindu tradition a circle represents the wheel of samsara, the cycle of life and death.

Circles are found in many natural forms and remind us of completeness, of beginning and ending all in one form. The image of a circle represents the wholeness of the universe available in the present, and the wholeness of the life and death cycle. Circles also suggest and give expression to serenity and completeness, again, the whole. Where is the beginning, where the end? Are they not indeed part of a continuum? Enso circles are expressions of spirit that transcend both technique and the written word.

> *You have noticed that everything an Indian does is in a circle, and that is because the power of the world always works in circles, and everything tries to*

be round… The sky is round, and I have heard that the earth is round like a ball, and so are all the stars. The wind, in its greatest power, whirls. Birds make their nests in circles, for theirs is the same religion as ours… Even the seasons form a great circle in their changing, and always come back again to where they were. The life of a man is a circle from childhood to childhood, and so it is in everything where power moves.
—Black Elk

Painting Enso is a spiritual practice, sometimes done daily for decades. Traditionally the artist spends time in meditation, then paints the circle in one breath with a single stroke of the brush. A meditation concludes the painting.

The brush is dipped into the shining liquid. With one breath, one continuous stroke, it arcs upward. Like the subtle moment when inhalation becomes

> *exhalation, there's an imperceptible pause at the pinnacle, and then the brush turns downward, slowly approaching where it began.*
> —Sherry Chayat

The artist, following meditation, in an act of courage, willingly confronts the emptiness of the blank paper, just as s/he has experienced the emptiness – the space – of meditation: nothingness. The instant the brush touches the paper, out of nothing comes something. This creation brings the possibility of beauty, as well as the inevitability of loss and consequent grief, for everything changes. The blank paper is no longer empty, and this is a loss. The circle itself, even as whole and solid as it appears, will change with age and time.

Detailed instructions for painting Enso circles may be found in *Chapter 12, Essence: Art* of my book *Essence: The Emotional Path to Spirit*.

I have used the painting of Enso circles to train volunteer grief facilitators and interfaith chaplaincy students, in university counselor education and to teach meditation to grade school students. Following a period of meditation, they practice drawing circles, continuing to maintain silence. Then I give everyone a special paper to use for their final painting. Still in silence, they paint their last circles. Afterwards, in the Gestalt manner, I ask each person to describe his or her spiritual life as a circle, that is, to speak as his or her circle. I hear comments such as, "I start out strong, then become gentle and quiet at the end"; "I look hard and smooth on the outside but I am rough and jagged on the inside"; "I have a thin skin but lots of room inside"; "I am as strong and protected and nobody can see inside"; "Though I look weak and thin, I am connected to myself with a certain fragile beauty."

[Reference: *Enso: Zen Circle of Enlightenment* by Audrey Yoshiko Seo; Weatherhill, Boston and London, 2007.]

Like countless days past and days future, here is this day, this day of all days is here now. You did not have to do anything to create this day, it is here for you simply because you are alive. It is here bringing you space and time, a place to live, a place to be.

In the coming of this day let there be the great silence that already is, just like the day itself. How full the silence of this day, even as minor sounds intrude. The silence, the background of eternal silence is always there, here. Allow the silence to expand...

Place yourself in the silence, a physical being in the vast silence. Notice who and what you are: flesh and bones, bones and flesh. Find yourself: your feet, your legs, your middle, your chest, your arms, your head.

Find and feel who you are physically and awaken.

Within this self find your feelings and bring consciousness to your feelings. No matter which of the many, only one at a time can come forth. So let it come up, this feeling, and out into the universe, then another, and so on.

Now there is space, room for what's underneath. Now your core, your essence has room, so give it permission to emerge. Your spirit is not separate at all. Be your spirit.

May you continue this day to be your whole self. Wherever you go this day, bring your whole being.

Your gift today is wholeness.

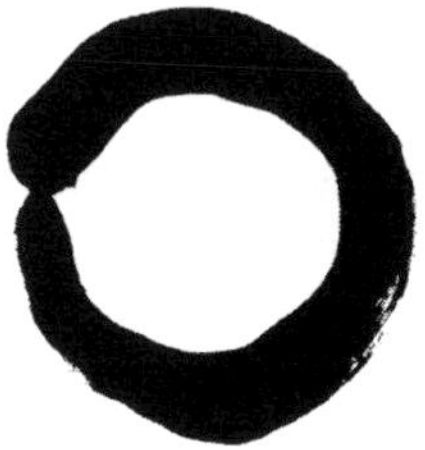

Welcome to the day that waits. No need to do anything. The day is here. It brings itself to you. Here you are, this day is yours with both its familiar habits and its extraordinary unknowns.

As the day waits, let silence reign, the silence of anticipation, then bring the silence home to the present, this very second. Second after second of silence. Let the thought intrusions come and go and you can return to the silence, over and over again…

Scan your body, bring the energy of awareness to each other part, first what you can see, the outside, and then the deeper, down to every cell. From your feet up your legs, calves, thighs, waist, chest, arms and head. Awaken with the vibration of awareness.

Next see what's there emotionally. There and here, present. What is it that you feel? Here it is. Let it grow as it wants, let it express, a word or sound coming out your skin and out your mouth.

Feel the space you create, the openness. Cleaner, clearer space for your spirit to breathe. Who you really are in this moment, and who you have always been forever. And who you will always be. That you is here now.

Be this timeless person alive in this second in this world and this world's day. May you only be who you have always been this day, nothing more, nothing less.

Your gift today is your uniqueness.

Enso Morning

Blessings and welcome to this day today. It is yours. The day has its own life just as you have your own life. It is another paradox: the day does not need you, yet there is no day without you. Of the many ways to live this lesson the most simple is: relax.

In this moment's relaxation breathe into the silence and make it large. Spread this silence out like a warm blanket over all that is here. Everything, absolutely everything is still existing and everything is still…

In this stillness you exist. Find the outline of your physical self, that boundary where you begin and end physically. Inhabit yourself from your feet up through your middle, your chest, your head. Be there and be here, in yourself.

You have a home here in yourself, a home now for your feelings. Allow your feelings to be at home, one at a time – the only way they can be. Give a feeling life and then expression. Go into it so it can come out. Connect with the rhythm of your feelings.

With the cycle of feelings happening, your spirit now is reassured it has room, space in which to live and to manifest. This deeper level is reached, is tapped and touched. Integration happens. So be who you are, spirit. No separation. Just you as spirit, spirit as you, totally unique, different. Your spirit.

May your whole entity hug itself to start out this day. Nothing can change who you are today, no person, no judgment, no action. May you have the courage this day to be who you are and, in addition, to develop the appreciation of how many other spirit selves are with you today.

Your gift today is connection.

This good and blessed morning greets you. Such newness; another opportunity, like it or not, to live with not knowing. The strongest years-old habit can be broken in an instant, voluntarily or involuntarily. Welcome to this new day.

There is no better place for unknowing than silence. Merge your not knowing into the quiet of this moment. Answer mental intrusions with "don't know" and let them melt away into the silence...

Gently come back to what you can know in the present and presence of your body. Shine the energy of your awareness on each part, skin and bones and down into the cells: feet, legs, waist, chest, arms, head and face. Awake slowly and with loving care.

Welcome your emotions to the day you have here. Find what lives in your belly and your heart and welcome the expression, which is all feelings want.

Now there is some emptiness that you need not fill right away. And this space summons spirit, allows your spirit to emerge. Spirit can live without filling, for spirit is always here anyway. Welcome your spirit. It is you.

May you go forth with your unknowing, as well as what you know about yourself, both.

Your gift is not knowing.

Welcome as this day dawns. Open to it through a child's eyes. Stay with the slight anxiety, which is really only energy, energy for this day of yours.

Be here in your new day in silence, the silence of creation. Let go of anticipation, the things of life, and be here in this silence, life itself…

Recognize that for now you live your life in this body, your temple this time. Notice it, feel it, inhabit it. Awaken it by feeling it now: your feet that ground you on this earth, your legs, your thighs, your belly, your chest, your arms to handle your world, your head and face, that give and receive so much.

Your emotions surface from the deep well, bubbling

up to be expressed into the universe. There is no stopping them. Like lava they burn their own path, one way or another. Do not resist them, but welcome your feelings.

As your feelings well up, so comes a second, deeper force. Your soul, that which is most you, you in purest from, now has the way clear. As basic as your breath, your soul is your life itself. Be your soul.

Enter this day open from the inside out. May you find the courage to be outside who you are inside, all one. May you bring your essence to the world today.

Your gift today is essence.

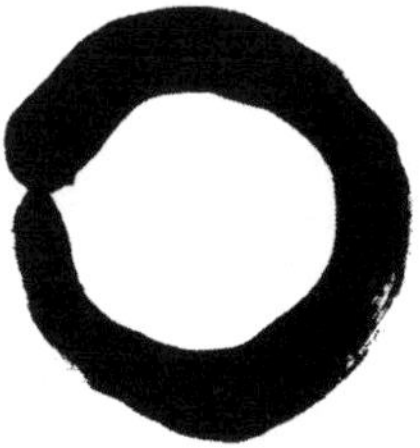

Here it is, this day, for you. And here are you in this day. Already and now. Your present. Your present of time and space for life. Allow yourself to open and receive what is freely given, naturally a gift. Accept the gift of this day.

Let this time of nothing to do have its silence. There really is nothing to do. You are being. Breathing naturally, existing. All and everything is here, moment after moment of silence, on and on forever…

How you begin to inhabit this day is with your physical self. Find it now. Touch it with your awareness. From the earth upwards, your feet, your legs, your middle, chest, arms and hands, then head and face. What will you face today?

Within the physical lies the emotional. Your feelings grow and search for expression outside in the world. Let only one emerge as only one can. Allow this organic emergence.

Having left the physical and emotional behind, now there is only spirit, that spark of light. Again, nothing to do. Even breathing takes care of itself. Today inhabit your essence and let your essence inhabit you.

May you go into this day yourself, as who you are. May you find this to be enough. When you decide to do so, may you offer yourself to others, to join your essence with theirs.

Your gift today is enough.

Open your eyes. Open everything, every part. Don't miss this day that is in front of you and inside you. Meet it and greet it. Meet yourself and greet yourself. Welcome.

Let this greeting now be in silence. Allow the soothing silence to wash ever gently toward you, over you, around you, and inside you...

Drop into yourself so you know and experience the living, breathing, physical being that you are right now. Feel and awaken your skin and bones, this marvelous structure, down to your marrow, your physical core.

Just as deep are your emotions. Encourage now your

feelings, give them energy, give them life. Welcome them, one at a time. One is not better than another, believe it or not. Your feelings must live so that you can live. Welcome your feelings.

As the way clears for your spirit it is like fog clearing under the warmth of the sun. Unclouded now, your spirit can live.

May you carry your spirit with you today. Indeed it is not even something to carry, for it is your spirit. Be who you are as you go forth into this day. Continue yourself.

Your gift today is continuity.

Meet this day. Ready or not, here it is. Introduce yourselves. Because the day is new you have an opportunity to be new as well. As new you are. Meet this day being the being you would like to be. The day doesn't know the difference and blesses you.

Bring new silence to your newness. Do not disturb the silence of the ages, but touch and inhabit this silence that has always existed and will always exist. Simply be in this spacious silence...

Slowly awaken your body. Scan your physical being toe to head, call forth attention and energy. Shine energy on your feet, legs, knees, thighs, waist, chest, arms, neck, face, and head.

After the physical comes the emotional self, all feelings, and all are acceptable, even useful. But only one feeling at a time. Give yourself permission to feel. Breathe so that your feelings have life. Encourage them to come here and give you life.

Clearing happens now, openness. Vast and expansive. Your spirit has room. Simply to be. Welcome your spirit as you welcome yourself, the same. Nothing to do but be who you are, spirit.

May you have all and be all you need this day. Feel the depth and breadth of who you really are. What more is there? Bless yourself and go forth.

Your gift today is space.

This day is an opening, an unfolding right in front of you. Nothing to do, the sun comes up on its own. So much life all around with you as part of it. You are assisted and welcomed to this day on all sides.

This help is subtle and quiet. The molecules of air surrounding you, supporting you, breathing you, going in and out of you, are silent. Be with this silence now…

Focus the energy of your awareness on your physical self. Bring the gentle heat of awareness to each part of your body, touching with attention, awakening your feet, legs, knees, thighs, waist, chest, arms and head, one at a time, reminding you of your body whole.

Your home is awake, that which holds your emotions. Give them your permission to awaken too. Feelings are looking for permission to live and express. Here they come, eager, one at a time. Feel one and feel the freedom of allowing it to come up and out.

Notice how the flowing creates a pathway for your spirit, an openness. Open to and open from your spirit. This is who you already are and still are today. So open, so easy to be who you are now.

May you go forth today open. May you remember you are a living organism, opening yourself to possibility.

Your gift today is flexibility.

Enso Morning

Blessed be this day. And blessed be all those who wake to this day, for without you there would be no day, blessed or not. It is you who greet this day that this day is for.

Here in the first time of this day, let there be silence to honor the beginning that comes, unbroken, as part of all the dawns since the beginning of time. Listen to the silence of creation…

In this silence find your physical self, here. This is your house, your temple, and your home for now, today. Find your feet, your legs, your waist, your chest, your arms, your neck, your head, and your face. Acknowledge this physical form that allows you to be in the world this day.

Seek and meet now your emotions. Whatever and whichever feeling it is, let it be and let it exist. Do you think you can do otherwise? Let the feeling come, as it will. Welcome your feeling, encourage it, and set the feelings in motion, one after another.

As the flow continues, the movement creates health and space for your spirit, your essence, to be seen and experienced. Give your spirit the breath of life. Your breath, fragile and involuntary, both comes from and expresses your spirit. Breathe life into your spirit.

May you continue to breathe your spirit as this day unfolds. Bring consciousness to the enormous history and momentum of your being. Continue yourself this day while in the company of so many others doing the very same thing, living this day.

Your gift today is momentum.

Welcome and tender blessings on you this new day. Here is yet another series of opportunities for healing. How many days have there been and how many days will there be? Of all the past days and of all the future days here now is this day. And you are here.

Some things happen only in silence. Against many odds, in spite of many encroachments, let there be silence in this brief time. Quiet right here. Strip away the layers of distraction. Hear your essence in the silence...

Tune yourself to feel your physical body. Existing in a physical world. Wounds happen. Blood is lost. Oil fouls beaches. And healing is needed. Scan your body and your world to find where healing is called for, and send your energy there.

Once repairs are begun, then feelings arise. "I'm wounded." "I hurt." "I am healed." Whatever the feeling, it begins to surface. Encourage your feelings, one at a time, even if quickly. Welcome that which gives you life. Open, externalize, express. Create an avenue for your life's healing.

It is like chopping through an ancient vine-encrusted jungle so that your spirit may have a path. Breathe down into your spirit; breathe it up into the air. Clear the pathway for your spirit to express who you are. Fresh. Today. Right now.

May you walk the paths you create for yourself this day. Give yourself the gifts of your own healings. Only then will you be able to offer them to others. Only then will you have the integrity to say, "Here, I have walked this path, and I am alive." May your wounds continue to heal.

Your gift today is healing.

Allow yourself to be blessed as you begin this day. Allow yourself to really take in the fact that you are blessed. There are many people, spirits and forces that bless you. Identifying them is not important. What is important is to receive your blessings.

Receive in silence. Let the silence itself flow toward you from all around, from everywhere, and enter every part of you. Soak up the silence. Receive the silence…

Notice that which is receiving, how solid you are compared to the silence, your body doing the receiving, this body that is home. Open your body from foot to head so it is awake to do all the sensing, all the receiving and giving today.

So too does it hold all your emotions. Let your bodily senses show you how you feel, and let there be no impediment, no barrier to feeling and expressing here and now what you find of your feelings.

As this expression happens, room opens, a cathedral is created, that sacred place inside, where you safeguard your spirit. Reminded now that your spirit will always be with you, allow it to expand. Give it what it needs to grow, as if you were a loving gardener. Tend your spirit.

May you remember today that many beings walk with you as you go through this day. They hold you and support your presence in the world today.

Your gift today is nurturing.

Blessings to you as you begin this day. Whatever you think is in store for you today, know that anything can happen. Let go of your plans; loosen their grip so that you have some freedom, so that you have some response-ability. After all, the day must be yours first before it can be anyone else's.

Loosen and relax now into silence. Join the stillness that surrounds you like the air itself. Become one with the all-pervading quiet, merge with it, become the stillness here...

Gradually let yourself become aware of your body and how it serves you. It has carried you through the night and it is about to carry you through this day. Notice it and nurture it from toes, legs, thighs, waist, chest, arms, and head; feed it in many ways.

Living in your body, now live in your emotions, and let them live in you. Life and health go together. Give life to your feelings. Welcome your feelings to the life of this day, right now. Express what you already feel in this moment.

Underneath the emotion lies the spirit, your spirit, and the unspoken definition of who you are. Lying there stretched out like a giant soft animal, your spirit seeks expression in your life. How can you be creative?

Go now into this day as a whole being, moved and motivated by your spirit. Instead of having a spirit, be your spirit. Remind yourself who you are underneath, down deep, wherein lies your essence. Express your spirit today.

Your gift today is creativity.

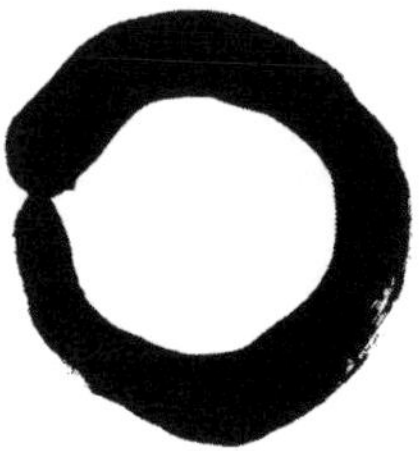

Welcome to this fresh, crisp new day, as yet unopened. May you too open as this day does, gently and with reverence. Allow yourself to feel precious, wanted and welcomed. As you are.

Let there be silence here and now, just some quiet time to feel yourself. The silence surrounds you, holds you in its embrace. Both smooth and textured at the very same time, this silence is tangible and alive, holding you…

Bring to your awareness now your physical body, that which gives you a home on this planet. It is your home within your larger home. Experience your physical self by tuning in and tuning up: your feet, your legs, your waist and middle, your chest, your arms, your face and head, and thus your whole.

In your self find your feelings. Reach in to meet your feelings, one at a time, and assist them, encourage them. As a shy child, they need a gentle and welcoming hand. Let one emerge, then later another and so on.

As feelings flow so will your spirit, for they use the same pathway. Breathe life into your spirit so that you can live being who you actually are. Live from your core out this day.

May you enter this day simple, and simply as yourself. Know and experience the gentle power of being yourself. Take with you this quiet confidence.

Your gift today is the strength of your gentleness.

Welcome from the universe, from the great spirit of all, from the powers that be. Why are you chosen to begin this day? Because there is no other. You are blessed to have consciousness as again the sun rises.

As you were chosen in silence, let the silence continue. This dawn, the newest of so many, unfolds now in the silence of creation, as consciousness continues…

Bring your attention now to your physical being and notice yourself, starting with your feet and moving slowly upwards. Notice where there is warmth. Notice where there is any discomfort and linger there. Focus your healing awareness on those places that are asking for it.

So too with your emotions. Simply see what's there, present. No need to judge: a feeling is a feeling, not you, but an emotion you are experiencing. Gently move from experiencing to externalizing.

Now your spirit has room to live, to be seen. All-pervasive and seeking expression, your spirit is moving, alive, as are you. Join. Be your spirit this day.

May you bring your consciousness with you throughout this day. Go with all your senses, including your intuition, awake and alive.

Your gift today is awareness.

Such an unknown is a new day, starting off dark with the shades drawn. Comfort and welcome to you who have the courage to face the dark and the light. Honor yourself for participating in this day. Whatever happens, you are here.

The dark makes no sound as it changes to light. Be with the silence and let it spread as the light spreads and grows, inside as well as outside. Inside and out, all quiet…

Slowly recognize your form, where you begin and end physically: your feet, legs, middle, chest, arms, neck and head. What you are materially wakes up and recognizes a being.

This container you are holds emotions, but only as a bird's nest holds its young. Escape is both life giving and inevitable. Encourage your feelings to take wing and fly.

There is something about expressing emotions that clears the way for spirit. Perhaps the air is stirred. Perhaps feelings are the leading edge of spirit forging its path. Let your spirit have wings.

Go into this day lightly. Though your body carries you, remember how much more you are than this, and let this show: be transparent.

Your gift today is having wings.

Join the day. Reflect for a moment on how many similar creatures are opening their eyes and beginning their days with you right now. Join me, and join the throng, to merge with so much energy.

Notice the silence against which all the noises are silhouetted as if in black. Return with me to the great background of silence. For this time, only the quiet, ancient background of silence is brought here to the foreground...

Be aware of the one who notices, your physical self using the five senses. Information is coming in from all sides and from within. See and feel and taste and smell and touch how you are physically from your toes to the top of your head, notice yourself.

Now do the same at the deepest emotional level. What are your senses telling you about your feelings? No judgments, only one feeling, then another, working its way up through time to awareness, to expression.

Soon here is your spirit emerging, to join other spirits, to remind you both who you are and what you are a part of. Offer your spirit.

Enter the great stream of the day. Join the countless others by simply being who you are, now and through the day and night.

Your gift is joining.

Welcome. When I stepped out onto the front porch to let the cat out, there in the morning light was a huge bright rainbow in the sky across the street, arching silently earth to earth. Unexpected, balanced, graceful, colorful and perfect, the rainbow welcomes us.

The silence of the rainbow was magnificent. Let silence now shine on you. Let the silence enter and shine its light inside, illuminating all the dark and gray places. Let the silence do its work…

Feel your physical self supported and held by your chair or couch right now. Allow yourself to be held as the container does what it was made to do. Feel your body held and supported by the earth.

Search your body for clues and beginnings of feelings. Notice the stirrings and stir them like a passionate cook. Taste your feelings, give them life and give them expression, sound or word.

Next, remember your innermost part, not even a part really but the whole you, deep, deep down and all around. Remember that which you have always been and always will be, your spirit. Remember.

Go forth steadily, balanced and sure-footed. Today may you keep your balance and feel anchored to your foundation, your essence. Be calmed and grounded.

Your gift today is balance.

Sleep is over. Breathing continues. Consciousness dawns. Before all the thinking begins, let yourself experience simply your ability to notice. Be a being of consciousness. What a precious ability: be conscious.

Stay inward for now and allow silence to reign. Be conscious of your breathing in this silence. Stretch the silence out, breath to breath, and notice the pause, deeply silent, between the breaths…

Breathe into your body to give it form, shape and substance. Move breath and awareness from your feet on upwards through legs, middle, chest, arms and head, breathing all the way.

Give the breath of life now to your feelings. Welcome

whatever you find for it is life itself. No judgments whether you find tenderness or rage, only life and some form of expression, simple acknowledgment and validation of who you are, now.

So comes the spirit, yours, the spirit of you. Quiet yet eager, spirit is breath too, every time you breathe. Find that place from which your spirit flows: from behind your eyes, from your heart. Breathe out your spirit. Go now into this day as yourself, conscious spirit.

May you notice yourself and give yourself this day, as you give yourself to this day.

Your gift today is breathing.

Welcome as the circle of life continues, heralded by yet another dawning. We have come again, miraculously, to another day, you and I. After the circle of sleep, here is the cycle of day, with its promise of participation.

Let the promise exist in silence. Silence is all promise, all fertile ground for what comes next. And now what comes next is more silence, the unending future brought into the present moment in silence...

Come home, be at home in your body, as it is, as you are. See how you can offer your physical self acceptance. Accept and honor your feet, your legs, your waist, your chest and arms, your head and face, as they are, without judgment, but with acceptance.

Bring this quality to your emotions too. Simply notice and accept what you feel now. Because you feel it, it is acceptable. Another miracle, but possible.

Your spirit is uncovered as if you took the blanket off the bed in the morning. Yes, your spirit may be difficult to define and sometimes to find, but remember you are always you. Remember yourself.

May you enter and proceed through the cycle of this day as a willing participant. Engage and contribute to the cycles of this day and of this life.

Your gift this day is participation.

Welcome to this new day. Sailing offshore out of sight of land, I watched hour after hour as the waves formed, peaked and melted away. Here is another day in which to form, peak, and melt.

Let any noise, inside or out, recede into the background so that silence comes forth into the present here. Feel the great quiet come from both the earth below and the sky above...

Find and feel your physical being. Notice the space that you occupy in the world, this way that you are in the world with your body: breathing, alive, and moving. Your feet, your legs, your middle, your chest, your arms and head, are all the expressions of you.

Feel your feelings stir and awaken. Perhaps it is some small tenderness, a flower bud forming, so fragile, paper-thin. Protect it, nurture this first feeling, whatever its source, whatever its name.

Some essence is birthing all the time with every breath. Help it along. There is integrity here, who you are. Encourage your spirit to come, to be present and to express. Let it shine through your eyes as you see and as you are seen today.

May you go into this day with the knowledge that you are like a wave in the ocean, a small brief part of something so vast that it stretches your imagination, so deep that you see yourself differently.

Your gift today is forming.

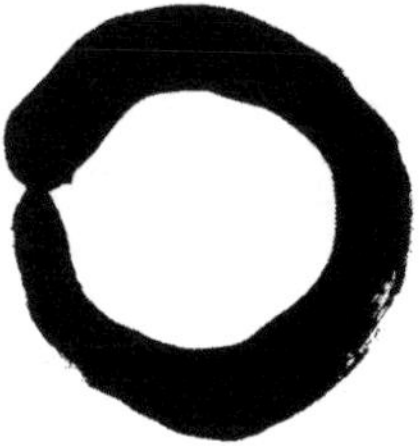

After a long night, or a short night, sleep or not, the day is here. Whether there will be rain and wind or sun and blue sky, the day is upon us. The earth, which seems so solid beneath our feet, turns through space offering another day.

Recently hiking in the western hills, when I paused to rest I stopped the gentle crunch of leaves underneath my feet. Silence took over. Let silence advance and surround you. Let silence fall around you like colorful leaves fluttering down from the trees overhead...

Feel the silence with your physical self, letting the quiet touch and penetrate your skin down to your bone and marrow. As you scan and awaken your body down from your head to your feet, give your physical being the energy of awareness.

Place your awareness into your emotions, whatever it is that you feel right now. Give yourself permission to really feel it and give the feeling an expression, a descriptive word, a sound.

In the same way, whatever your soul is right now can come forth and manifest. Here is a chance for your soul, as ancient as it may be, to birth itself anew. Just as the earth turns and the leaves fall, your soul moves through its seasons intact and wants only acknowledgment.

Move into this day then with your parts joined, whole. Remember who you are, part of the patterns and seasons. Join the ebb and flow of the hours and minutes of this day.

Your gift today is change.

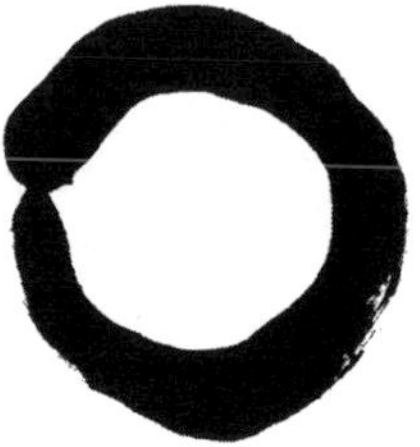

Welcome home. Be welcomed to this day at hand. Be in the day effortlessly, without having to make it happen. The earth turns by itself, creating this fresh morning, this fresh time and space for you.

In my house silence is easiest at night while the people and animals of the city sleep. Hold on to the silence for a while longer, keeping it wrapped around you like a fine cloak. Do nothing but breathe...

After being out of your body for the night, return to your body now. Come and be at home. Feel yourself, your feet on the earth, your legs, middle, your chest and arms, and head and face. Begin to stretch and move out into the day.

As you come from the background of sleep's unconsciousness, let a feeling emerge into the foreground. Right now I feel curious. What feeling will the very next moment bring? More of the familiar pattern or some unexpected feeling?

Do you know your soul? After the firestorm or flood of feelings what is there but the quiet of essence? Come be at home in this new and ancient way. Again there is nothing to do but be with yourself at the deepest level.

May you go out and meet the day whole, alive and eager to experience what you find. Let there be familiarity as you encounter other souls wandering through the day.

Your gift today is homecoming.

Hello. Hello to this day. After the tangled, mysterious and half-remembered world of night dreams, here we are in this world, to begin again. Because we cannot really be in one place until we have left the old, thank the dream world, knowing you can return tonight, and arrive in the day world.

Let this day begin now in silence, as so many events have begun. Yet this is not the silence of anticipation. This silence lives on its own, has its own identity and its own power, a quality unlike any other. Allow this silence to live...

Notice now who you are physically, as you sit here. Right now there is little movement save your eyes scanning these words. Become conscious of the space your body takes up. You are form and substance in space, from your toes to the top of your head.

Our emotions too take up space, just as much, as they are found, conceivably, anywhere in our body. Find your feeling, just one to start with, and give it the life of awareness, no matter which feeling it is, or where in your body you find it.

Underneath all there is something so deep, so powerful, so constant, that we forget that it requires time and expression. This, our spirit, not only describes who we really are, but also connects us to the ancient past, as well as suggests ways to join other spirits in the present.

Leave the old, these last minutes, and venture outward into the new, this very moment. Find the courage to leave the familiar shore and sail into uncharted waters this day.

Your gift this day is courage.

May you enter this day with gratitude. No matter your age, so much has already happened: people, events, sun, rain, nights and days; all the past propels us to this moment, the moment of a new day. It is like the fine dew on the morning grass that awaits your step.

Hold your first step a while longer and be in silence. Even as a single leaf swings gracefully and slowly to join its comrades on the ground, let yourself fall quietly into meditation. Swing gracefully down in to yourself…

Once home, feel the solidity of your body. This is your shape and form. Right now, find some appreciation for all that your body is and does for you, as it expresses you in earthly form. Appreciate yourself, from your feet and legs, up through your waist and chest to your arms, neck and head.

Now locate that single feeling, out of all those floating down like that leaf. Find it and protect it on its way. Relief, anger, grace, love, sadness – whatever it is – honor it and express it, for then you express yourself.

And now down deep, encounter your essence, lying patiently under all distractions. Everything comes and goes, even life itself, while your essence survives day to day, past and future.

Join me and all the others as we enter this day. Do so with the ease of a leaf enjoying its lazy journey earthward, as it floats to its new home.

Your gift today is grace.

Welcome. Up before daylight dawns and before the heat comes and before the newspaper arrives brings the question: what do all these events have in common? They are all manifestations of the great life force of which we are a part. Join.

Let the life force exist around you in silence now. Life continues with all its forces both outside you and inside you. Locate that still, deep place – like an underground pool – inside you. Silence…

Bring your consciousness up to your body so that you awaken your physical self, all the complexities and functions of your body. Start at your feet and move up to your legs, middle, chest, arms and head, awakening as you go.

What emotions are you aware of right now? Bring both consciousness and acceptance to whatever feeling you find. Even the smallest as-yet-undefined feeling is acceptable. It asks only for your help and validation, nothing more, nothing less.

Then there is no barrier to the life force. Let it flow forth as an expression of who you are, your spirit. Let your spirit flow and show.

May the profound energy of life itself empower you this day. May you find many ways to express who you are today.

Your gift today is the life force.

A gentle welcome this morning. Pace yourself slowly and tenderly into this new day. It is such a journey from the depths of sleep to full wakefulness. I often want to prolong the journey so that I can receive the beginnings of the day without the template I usually wear, but fresh, newly minted.

Let nothing disturb the lack of noise; create silence. You don't have to start anything. You are already breathing and that is all that is necessary. Silence fills all the space around you and melts inside…

Inside you the dark, warm, juicy organs do their work, do what they are made to do, they give you life for another day. Offer your appreciation to all your unseen physical self. Send your thanks down deep to the marrow of yourself and spread it throughout your body.

Down there somewhere your emotions move. Usually they rest; now let them be restless. There is health in movement, life in expression. Encourage your feelings up to the light of day, to express in sound and word.

So too does your spirit desire expression. Coming up from your past, all that you ever were, your spirit leaks through every pore, out to form your aura, or your invisible (to some) signature.

May you be who you already are this day. Be with a minimum of masks and charades. Let yourself show.

Your gift today is juice.

Open your eyes to this coming day. Remember that what you see outside is but a reflection of what you are inside. Help the world welcome you today by seeing the world. Actively project receptivity from your eyes; take in the world.

Receive silence in these next moments of today. Soak up the silence that exists in between all the little and not-so-little noises of today's beginnings; the silence is always there, waiting. Now let it be here with you…

With your mind's eye scan your physical being. Use your attention to bring life to your body, to your feet and legs, to your waist, to your chest and arms, to your neck and head. Especially open your eyes so that today they may both give and receive.

See what feelings you have. Use your perception to find any feeling, even the ones that hide in lightless corners. Open your vision to your feelings.

We humans yearn for unobstructed views, to mirror what lies within. When I sit on Maine's rocky shores, my spirit leaps out through my eyes and is affirmed by the limitless expanse; horizons beckon our spirits.

May you go into this day with your eyes open, and find others to meet your gaze. See how you might let yourself be seen; allow yourself to be seen through your eyes, your windows.

Your gift today is vision.

A new morning is here, a new day, ready or not. Since we can't stop the earth from revolving around the sun, we don't have a choice about whether or not a new day dawns, only what we do with it, how we live it. Welcome to a million choices.

Choose silence right now, as much as you can. In my silence now I can hear the cawings of crows in the distant background. I can't see their black feathers, but the sounds splash like distinct drops of water on a smooth pond, holes in the silence that quickly mend…

Tune in to your body. Feel the beat of your heart sending blood throughout your body, down to your feet, starting back up through your legs, waist, chest again, then arms, neck and head.

Who knows exactly where feelings start? What is important is to ease their way, to keep the river flowing. Obstacles appear like boulders. Of course. The river of feelings may be diverted, even dammed up for a while. But always feelings work their way through to release.

Deep underneath the surface turbulence lies still water, dark, primitive. Underlying everything, close to the core and full of mystery, the soul slumbers like a hibernating Loch Ness creature. What disturbs your soul's sleep?

May you leave sleep behind you today. May you welcome the flow of your feelings to the surface, so they flow around the barriers to expression.

Your gift today is choice.

Enso Morning

One tree welcomes me when I step outside, its golden sunlit leaves like some ancient treasure find. The gold tree stands tall shining in the pale morning light, and says but for you I am not seen. Thus I was given an important task.

As the tree stands in silence, let your silence shine. Be like a tree, rooted, spreading into space without a sound. Spread quiet from every pore. Give off silence into the world, move it out to all the space around you so that it fills the room…

Sit here, and feel the space that you fill and fill it more. Know that this is your space. Offer your body the comfort of a home. Send appreciation to your feet, legs, waist, chest, arms and head, and together to your whole physical being.

Emotions take up space too and if not acknowledged become coalesced like petrified wood. Grant yourself now permission to breathe life into your feelings. Awareness of your feelings can be permission enough; awareness is enough for now.

However you define your spirit at this moment, let it shine like gold. Whatever this essence is, however you imagine it, breathe it and express it, let go of the definitions. Let yourself shine at this moment.

Begin to move yourself into this day, breathe and stretch, make paths in the air. Take your whole affirmed self with you, like a light shining forth.

Your gift today is luminosity.

Welcome. However we measure time, the sun has come around again. When we leave the unconsciousness of sleep we leave the darkness of night. Consciousness and light are given to us with the new day. Accept these gifts offered you.

Accept in silence what is offered in silence. When I walk in the deep woods beside the marsh I am surrounded by brown leaves, each one silent. Each one silently says its name to me: "Change," "Change," "Change." Silent change…

Be with your body now while it breathes. Breathe in and out taking in new air, letting go of the old. Take in the air; take it down to your toes. Bring fresh energy to every part of your body: legs, waist, chest, arms and head.

Remember, the word emotion has to do with movement. Emotions need to move, move around, move up, and move out. Right now notice what you are feeling and give it some movement. With movement comes life, the expression of life.

Once feelings stir, the soul is not far behind. Whether it is the passion behind the anger, or the tenderness behind the sadness, your depths give up essence. Something fundamental has changed when you offer your soul.

May you create ways this day to live in your passion and your tenderness both. Remember it takes more energy to repress who you are than it does to express who you are. May you be passionate, may you be tender.

Your gifts today are the leaves of change.

Welcome to this moment, to these moments and to the moments that stretch out in front of us this day like a path. Despite the distance between all of us we have these moments in common.

Let these distances shrink now in the communion of silence. Shared silence has an extraordinary quality of togetherness. Quiet down, quiet now, from the inside out and farther, as your silence reaches out and stretches out to all of us...

Slowly bring your awareness to your body. Use your five senses to harvest information about your physical self. Now send care, support and nurturing back to your body. Move a leg, change your back position, shift your weight, stretch a finger, and create ways to nurture your body.

Shrinking and expanding count as feelings. Sometimes I want less of the outside world and want everything to shrink. Sometimes I want more and want everything to expand. Find which of these you feel and find a way to express it.

Whatever feeling comes, another soon follows it and then eventually a different quality emerges. There is something in a tear that the soul loves. Or passion. Experiencing a deep feeling expressed, the soul says, "Ah," in deep understanding and appreciation.

Come, join with others as you walk into the day today. Come along farther down the path of your life. Let yourself see how your path is prepared for you just as the high trees give all their leaves to make a carpet for my long, wooded walks.

Your gift today is a path.

Welcome friend. Let the greeting penetrate, so you are able to welcome others you meet this day. And you can welcome each other from a deep inner place.

Continue welcoming yourself, now in silence. Let any sounds recede, let silence emerge here. Add a quiet moment to a quiet moment. As thoughts come, let them go. Let go over and over again, always returning to the silence that waits patiently...

Find your body, your home here, what you have in common with all humanity. Right here give loving attention to each part: feet, legs, waist, chest, arms, head, and thus wake up and love the whole, your whole physical being.

Move this process deeper. Attend to your emotional body; bring energy, acceptance and expression to your feelings. Greet what you find as you would a long-lost dear friend. You would welcome her and encourage her to tell her story. Let your feelings tell their stories.

Long ago on a Maine island, a friend of mine embodied friendship by treating me, right then and there, as though I were the person I dearly wanted to be. He saw through me right down into my soul, and we related soul to soul. Show your soul.

May you befriend yourself today and therefore be available to both yourself and your friends, old and new.

Your gift today is friendship.

Welcome. A place to start. We each have so many familiar patterns and events to welcome us. Even a non-welcome can be familiar. Allow the life you have created to welcome you, like slipping on a friendly old pair of blue jeans.

The silence waits for you too. Put on the silence and feel its familiarity and comfort. Sit with silence; remember that all day long it is nearby, waiting and available to you...

I sit here in my body, and you in yours, feeling certain parts of myself that are touching the floor, supported by the chair, each part reminded of itself and its function by physical contact. The connections bring reminders of life.

When the willingness to feel finds a feeling on its search, the feeling is contacted and awareness begins, the first step toward expression and healing. Again, no matter what the feeling, extend your welcome to it.

So too with your soul. Your willingness to acknowledge your depth and breadth connects you to the universe, to all those who have come before and all those who are yet to come. You are already connected.

Go into this day with the knowledge of your place, with the knowledge that you have a definite place in the world. Everything you do, like pulling on that old pair of blue jeans, everything you are, reminds you that you are home.

Your gift today is contact.

Behold a new day. Another day for the dance between solitude and communion. I enter this day a refugee from the isolation of deep dreams: no one knows where I've been but me. Only when I speak and act can I share and join.

Dance to silent music now. Your heart supplies the rhythm. The tune varies like the weather, which too is mostly silent. Let the silent melody of life overtake you, carry you into further silence…

I sit here writing, growing again into my body for a new day. Come back into consciousness and flood your body with awareness so that you are known to yourself: from toe to head.

Now is the time for fine-tuning. Though sometimes feelings are on the surface and obvious, often we must pause, take some time, like right now, to extend a welcoming hand to our feelings. What song wants to be sung? What sounds or words need to be expressed?

When the music comes from the very deepest place, it is the soul singing. Sometimes I feel so vulnerable that I am afraid I'll die if anyone hears my song; other times I play my sound from the mountaintop. Today?

May you contact inside the place that is most you and, when you choose, sing it out to the world. Create tune and lyric as only you can. Give voice to yourself this day.

Your gift today is your song.

Enso Morning

Greetings. Let everything that has already happened this day welcome you here. Even the small things, and especially the events that have not been perfect, want you to be here.

My silence doesn't start out very quiet, but gradually the outside noise fades into the background, and my inside noise begins, and very slowly it too melts away. Eventually I realize the silence wants me…

When you tune into your body it's a challenge to give every part equal attention. There is a sore spot here, an ache there, and an itch right here. But health needs energy too. Stretch, open and awaken every part of yourself from feet on upwards.

So too do your quiet emotions require honoring. Underneath lie the quiet feelings seldom expressed but which provide your foundation: what gives your life meaning. Feel these feelings.

Deeper still, your spirit lives at your core. With the crunch of everyday life it can be such a challenge to find spirit and push, pull, provoke, seduce, demand, allow it to surface. But it's a challenge that offers life.

May you experience new ways today of the world wanting who you are.

Your gift today is being wanted.

Welcome. This day begins to touch you as you begin to touch this day. Let the day reach out to you. Even with all the specifics unknown there is a willingness to begin the day. Join the day already in progress.

Underneath everything there is silence. Sitting here in meditation I can be as still as a mountain lake. All the streams of my life for these moments flow down the mountain slopes and come to rest, smooth and silent...

Except for brief moments when we defy gravity we are always touching something of the earth. Bring awareness to what your body is touching. Feel the contact, all of which leads back and down to the earth and to other people. Touch the earth. Touch other people.

We use the phrase: I am touched. What emotion is touching you right now? Allow yourself to be touched and affected by emotions, and continue the movement of feeling through you to expression.

In these beginning moments, drop down to find your essence. Take this time to consider who you are. Make contact with yourself. Renew the acquaintance. Join and rejoice when you find yourself.

May you touch the world today. May you let the world touch you. Be like a bold explorer of space and make first contact with a new world today.

Your gift today is touch.

Enso Morning

Welcome as the sunlight travels across the earth to bring us this day, given to us by the rotation of the planets. Receive this gift brought by ancient forces.

Such immense force comes in silence. All the hot fury of the sun muted not by distance, though perhaps by clouds, arrives here quietly. Join the silence of the sun, muted or not, and melt into your meditation…

Soak up the coming energy with your body; let it into your pores, into your skin and muscles, down to your very marrow. Receive this day's fresh energy, fill and fill yourself until you have accepted all you think you deserve, and accept more.

Receiving so much will likely spark a feeling. Breathe

into this sign of life, kindle and protect this tiny flame so that it burns away cobwebs and reaches for more air. Fan the flames of your feelings so they crackle quietly or roar loudly.

When the smoke clears what remains is burned pure, a core, miraculous. What not only can survive but also can strengthen is spirit. When I follow the fires in my life, the vocabulary of my life changes. My spirit teaches me a new language.

May your travel today, whether a few inches or across the continent, be full of sparks.

Your gift today is fire.

Welcome to this day. Join this day as naturally as rivulets join together in reflecting pools, then flow down through the pebbles and under the leaves. And as the water moves towards the ocean it deepens and confirms the choice of route, carving its way to the sea.

Now begin with a few seconds of silence, a mini-meditation, so easy these first few seconds. Create this path of silence choosing only stillness. Distractions come, distractions go. Temptations come, temptations are followed, and temptations go as you return to the natural path of silence, always there, always reflecting who you are...

Let your emotions be fluid. Seek natural movement of natural emotions. All night I slept lightly hearing the raindrops landing on the leaves on the roof. Countless drops, even in sleep, like feelings, each one a little different, and each one important.

Know your body, alive and solid, yet mostly water and thus fluid too, full of juice. Bring the light of awareness to your physical self, touching each area with energy, your feet and legs, thighs and waist, chest and arms, neck and head.

And way inside lies the deep pool of spirit, sometimes silver like mercury, that always seeks its own level and always is eager to escape. Whether we give it permission or not, our spirit shows and shines, attracts light, and reflects itself to other spirits.

May you find light today to both warm and reflect your spirit. And may the light make your spirit grow and shine. See yourself in the glow of spirit everywhere.

Your gift today is reflection.

Enso Morning

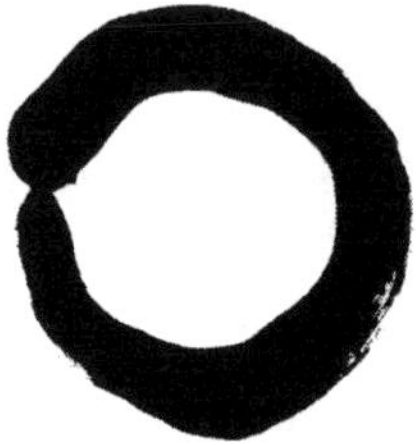

In these first few moments of the new day, let the world greet you. My old black male cat ambles up to me first thing this morning. He rubs his long furry length along me, and encourages me to pick him up and carry him into the day.

With the drop in temperature the early morning silence is crisp. The white frost made no sound as it crept in overnight. Continue this quiet time. Let it creep through your whole body, filling every space...

Notice the space you occupy with your body. Fill it and feel it. Feel your toes and feet and legs. Feel your midsection and chest. Feel your arms and head, especially your arms. Familiarize yourself with your body as you would your home after being away.

In what room of your body do your emotions live? When you find the dwelling place of your emotions you find the feeling itself. Simple awareness itself is healing – just to know. All that remains is to give the feeling some expression.

And all your spirit requires is a little awareness. It's not so much that you have a spirit, but that your spirit has you. You are spirit. You exist across space and time. When a friend thinks of you early in the morning, he or she calls forth your spirit, and there you are.

May you pick up this day as you might a friendly old cat. Both some tender stroking and healthy respect might be necessary.

Your gift today is arms.

Welcome. Consider how many events and people you will encounter today, all of them having some impact on you and you on them. Allow your five senses to wake up and open so that you will be able to harvest all that awaits you today.

Have a time of meditation now. Close your eyes to close off distractions and focus on your inner senses. When thoughts come, as they will, let them slide away. Drop down into yourself as a pebble drops into a lake and slowly sinks down through the layers of water to the very bottom...

From this meditative state gently bring the attention of your senses to your physical being. As you touch the parts of yourself with the energy of awareness, you bring wholeness and unity, as if you are stitching yourself together like a quilt.

Just as the time of year reminds us to harvest the fruits of the season, so is it healthy to harvest our emotions, also the fruits of hard work, time and natural growing processes.

In everything that grows there is the spark of life, a spirit that breathes life to keep the spark lit. When I see people who are experiencing a crisis or tragedy they tell me that their spirit is wounded. All help is to heal the spirit.

May your spirit have an abundant harvest this day, gathering what you need to keep your spark bright and shining.

Your gift today is gathering.

Just as the sky is revealed when the trees shed their leaves, allow yourself to see and welcome what is underneath the veil of illusion. Though often hidden by buildings, leaves, clouds, or our own lack of seeing, the sky is always there.

Let silence reign now, not merely the silence of anticipation but the silence of the present moment, alive, meaningful and challenging all by itself. This is what we have: this silent moment, and another, and another...

Later now, become aware of your body sitting here, being silent. Move your feet, feel your legs, your midsection, then, and your chest. Move your arms, hands and fingers. Stretch your neck and move your head. Open your eyes anew. Even sitting you can wake up your body.

Feelings too are obscured by what is on the surface, like a far blue sky hidden by brown leaves. And as the seasons of your life and the rhythms of the day move through their natural cycles, feelings are revealed. Illusions fall away, bringing clarity.

Seen with different senses, spirit connects us all. When you stop to think of or feel someone in the next room or across the country, it is your spirit that reaches out to them, that touches them. Know that you are touched by more spirit than you imagine.

May you this day see under the surface and beyond the distractions. May the true nature of your life be available to you, to own, to reflect on, and to enjoy.

Your gift today is sight.

A new day. Whether it feels like a miracle or a curse, it is here. It's such a human dilemma to struggle sometimes to accept the inevitable! Call up for this moment the images of your ancestors, spirits from the past, and accept their best wishes as you begin this day.

These spirits come in silence, of course. Let them bring the silence of the ages with them. Weave together the silence and the goodwill of your ancient people into a blanket of comfort. Wrap it around you...

Feel yourself held and warmed. Your blood sends this energy throughout your whole body, up from your feet to your legs and middle, then to your chest and arms, and neck and head, then around again, circulating life.

I look at the brown photograph of an ancestor and wonder what he was feeling the moment the picture was snapped. Surely he felt sadness in his life, and anger, and ecstasy, like me. Sharing blood we share emotions.

And much of what links us is spirit. Yes, there is mystery about spirit, yet communion too. Let go of the fierce need to know, and allow the fierce passion of spirit.

May you carry on the family, now in your own way. Be supported and strengthened by all those who have gone before. It is your turn.

Your gift today is your past.

Welcome to you this day. Even in the chilly morning the sun's rays bring warmth along with the light. Wavelets smaller than my little finger curl and break on the strong shore over and over again, and lap up the beach where I sit watching.

These waves, even though Spain is on the other side of their ocean, make little noise here; what sound there is has a melodious pattern that lulls me inward to my own breathing, in and out, in and out…

What notices everything is physical, all our senses housed in a body. Honor your house by bringing appreciation to your physical self, noting the parts of which you are made: your flesh and bones, your inner organs, your brain and eyes, your nose and mouth.

Appreciate your emotions too, coming as they do in endless waves of feeling. First consciousness is a flat empty surface, then a ripple that comes from a source sometimes known – a thrown stone or a busy storm – then the wave builds and eventually spills itself on the shore.

Deep underneath move the currents of spirit, sometimes dark and mysterious, sometimes light and musical. Know and remember that your spirit is there, here, always moving, informing your life, and seeking the sunlight of your expression.

May you gather yourself gently but powerfully to move into this day, using the natural ebb and flow to come and go through the day as you choose.

Your gift today is waves.

Hello. My big black cat knows I'll soon sit down in the maroon chair to write, so he waits until I settle in, then jumps carefully up and quickly arranges his long body to fit the curves of my lap. See how you can fit yourself to the curves of this brand new day.

Rest in silence for a few moments. Certainly let your body rest and offer rest to your mind, that hyperactive twin. It is astounding, shocking, how vehemently and often the mind turns down the gift of peace. Nothing to do literally but keep offering: here, here is peace...

Where you focus your attention you bring energy, heat and life. Put your attention on each part of your animal body, past the surface down to the cells. Own who you are so that you become whole and one with yourself and energized.

Take time right now to wake up your primitive emotional self. What feeling is it that is already here, alive and wanting acknowledgment and expression? It has a name, a noun to describe it. Use the language and speak the name of the feeling, a first step.

How do you envision the non-material world? Reflect for a moment here on all that you cannot see or touch. As I write I reach out to you through the realm of spirit. Consider how your spirit can wake up today and seek out other spirits.

May you simply be yourself today, and be flexible enough to fit the contours of the day as it unfolds. May you trust your instincts and follow your intuitions.

Your gift today is animals.

Morning is here and with the morning comes the day. This day begins to reveal itself. Outside there are no leaves left to hide the brightening sky. The clouds, silver and bright shimmering shades of gray, stand revealed and available.

The shimmering clouds reveal their beauty in silence, as if the silence itself is what communicates their majesty. Join this silence coming from above; partake of its splendor and hold it to you…

Hold yourself and feel what you are holding, this body of yours. Yours alone, it gives you a home here on this planet. Remember your place right now. Visit each part with appreciation, from your feet on the ground to your head in the air.

Gently let what obscures your feelings drop away like a cloud melting. Find the curiosity and courage to see what is there, to feel it. Know that what you find is not new and deserves to be revealed.

As the veils drop away like leaves past their prime, something deeper is glimpsed, substance without form, essence without matter. Yet it is essence still.

May you use your vision today to see what is here in front of you, and all around. And as you discern what was hidden, don't overlook the obvious.

Your gift today is revelation.

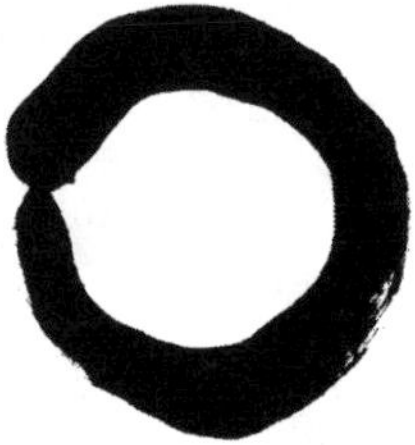

Welcome. Even as the day begins with the rising of the light here we know that on the other side of the planet darkness has come and the day is ended. So let us unfold in the new light of this precious day.

White, fragile and graceful, bubbles created upstream float silently downstream with the current. Be like a bubble floating on the surface, down an endless stream of consciousness, serene and noiseless...

Now remember your body, that which watches and breathes. Feel your breath enter and leave. Imagine it bringing fresh air and new energy to every part of yourself, circulating, stirring up, energizing.

Notice what is stirred up emotionally, what floats to

the surface. What comes up, as it leaves the darkness and comes to light, is what must come up. Welcome the inevitable.

Your spirit may not always show, but it is always there under the surface, in the depths. So, again, stir it up, bring your spirit to light today. Don't be afraid to see what happens when you show who you really are.

May you float with the currents of this day. Ride the stream: appreciate the rest offered by the eddies and enjoy the rush of fast water.

Your gift today is streams.

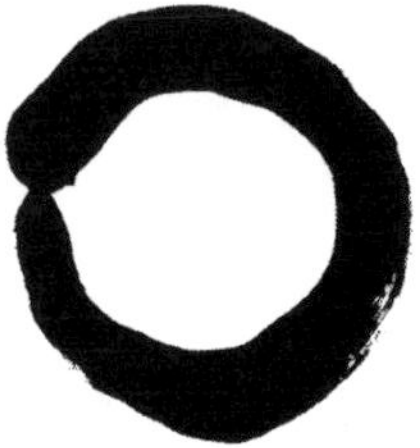

Here is the day. May whatever your five senses and intuition pick up please and welcome you. And may you welcome what you find as you begin the day. The grace and beauty available can be reflected in you.

A flat salt pond at the beach held by textured rocks reflects the sky in total silence. Imagine this silent reflection and bring it into your being. Be like a pool of water resting in the earth's arms...

Hold yourself. Find a way, literally or figuratively, to wrap your arms about yourself. Feel your own embrace around your shoulders, pressing and holding, around your legs, pressing and holding, caring.

Emotionally speaking, everything counts: whatever

the feeling, whether you like it or not, it is valuable simply because it is your feeling. Angst or humor, pain or pleasure, all it seeks is life, just like you.

Under these pools, in the darker depths, lies something often nameless. Shy but powerful, fresh but ancient, your spirit lives at the core underneath, to inform and influence everything.

May you feel the influence of your spirit today; may you allow others to feel it also, so that you create deep connections.

Your gift today is to see under the surface.

Welcome. Join this day. The earth continues to turn and light comes our way again. See how you can enter into the enormous life force we all share. Like the mile-wide river I drove across recently, nothing can stop the flow to the ocean.

Let your life quiet and flow in silence right now. Breathe in through your nose and out through your mouth. Bring in the fresh air, use all that it offers, then let go, all the way, of all you have used: the life cycle in miniature, every inhale, every exhale...

Focus now on your physical self, the one doing the breathing. This is your physical presence on the planet, again today as every day of your life. Remember it makes a difference to you and to others how you take care of and what you do with your body.

So too with your emotional body. Lately I have had emotional conversations with friends, in person and over the telephone. Each time feelings surge up like a wave breaking on the shore. Each time feelings need feelings to splash together creating a new sea.

This process of joining is communion, whereby individual souls join one another to create something greater, stronger and deeper. After emotional sharing a quality lingers that cuts across space and time. Something sacred is born.

May you today find the sacred in your life. May you be able to share what you find with another. And may you therefore create communion.

Your gift today is the sacred.

Welcome to this space in between night and day. Sometimes like today, it is gray as dark turns to light. This is the in-between time, a time to pause briefly and acknowledge the transition, and especially the twin feelings of loss and anticipation that come with any transition.

Infuse this pause with silence. Soak this time with the motionless presence of stillness. As we screen out distraction a kind of implosion takes place, inward, inward we travel, bringing silence to our innermost being...

As you come slowly out of your silence, come to your body. Bring consciousness to your physical form. Wake your body up: your feet, your legs and middle. Wake up your chest, arms and head. Wake up your face: stretch, wiggle, and make different faces for yourself.

Likewise, try on different feelings to find the one that is accurate for this moment. Is it annoyance and anger? Is it grief and sadness? Is it ecstasy and lightness? Let honesty decide so that the true feeling is acknowledged and expressed.

What never sleeps is spirit, though we may think it is sleeping. But even when our body is asleep our spirit roams, to influence and affect others, and ourselves. Right now, pause to think of a friend and invite their spirit to visit you. Notice that it happens instantaneously.

May you move through the many pauses and transitions of this day with grace.

Your gift today is time to pause.

Join the day; the invitation to you is open-ended. Join whenever and however you wish. Just as the waiting earth easily receives these delicate snowflakes of the first snowfall, so does the day receive you.

The white snow fills the air, dropping slowly in absolute silence. Let silence drop gently around you and fill you so that there is room for nothing but stillness...

After a while remember your body. Come back to the vessel that holds your earthly presence. Bring life to each part, starting with your feet on the ground, up through your legs and middle, to your chest, your arms and hands, handling your world, and finally your neck, head and face.

Investigate how you hold your emotions. Are your feelings content to be quietly held, or does one want more and move toward expression? What is its name and how can you give it birth right now?

The quality of spirit is that while it underlies and connects everything it is always seeking new ways to express. And here is the clue: any creative act is an expression of spirit, from a look across a table to cooking a meal to writing a letter.

May you create this day for yourself and for the other people in your life as effortlessly as the snowflakes drift down to the earth.

Your gift today is ease.

Best wishes this day. Overnight every bush, tree and blade of grass has grown a new skin of glistening glass. With the morning light every form shines as its true beauty is at last revealed.

The sparkling new world emerges from the dark of night silently. There is no sound to distract attention from the wonder. It is easy to join this silent wonder...

Whether it is the rigid forms of man-made structures or the more graceful forms of nature, we are one with the material world. After sleep grow again into your body and awaken yourself feet first, all the way up to your head.

What emotions are growing inside you, making their

way to the surface? Honor both their origin and their presence now. Find a way for a feeling to emerge before it becomes a real emergency.

Imagine a world where everyone's best self shines like crystal, beautiful essence revealed for all to see. The more you know about who you really are, the easier it is to let it show, and to look for essence in others, today.

May you show your true beauty today, in whatever form and expression you choose. Remember how much is already available; we must only open our eyes and see.

Your gift today is beauty.

As all the dreams and events of the night rush into the past where they belong, blessed be the present of this new day. Whatever has happened to you, years ago and yesterday, has propelled you to this very moment. Welcome.

When we leave behind the tumultuous history of all our prior years, we come to the pinpoint of the present in a grateful silence. Life is new. Let each moment now unfold in the enormous quiet of creation, moment after magic moment…

In the quiet of the house when I walk around then sit to write, my muscles creak and stretch, shooing away the cobwebs that sleep brought. Move and stretch in your mind then in your body. Bring blood and energy to every part, top to bottom.

Emotions run deep, unseen, but powerful nonetheless. We don't see the earth revolving through space either. Best to find a way to let the emotional currents surface, one at a time in their due course, as a river keeps flowing.

Also invisible is spirit, but for its countless manifestations, like yourself, like all of us. How might the part of you that is most deep, most pure, and most you, manifest this very day? To ask the question brings close the answer.

May you make yourself more visible today, so that you yourself may see who you really are.

Your gift today is magic.

You greet this day as a dry plant soaks up the rain. For it is you that gives this day life and meaning. You bring uniqueness and freshness to the day that would otherwise be absent. Your special eyes see the new day.

It is only when the rain lands and hits something that you hear it. Let there be silence now, the silence of rain falling before it lands. Allow the rain of silence to fall around you and inside you, washing away all thought and leaving you deeply clean…

What would feel the rain land? Walking in the wet woods I only notice the rain on my head after it has soaked through my hair. Imagine rain touching and waking up every part of your body. Refreshing.

When you invite your emotions to come up to the surface, does it matter if you don't like what you find? Give whatever feeling you have a name and some kind of expression. Remember you thus join a community of feeling people.

We humans have more that connects us than keeps us apart. What we have in common is spirit, a quality both unique and universally similar: the deeper you explore inside yourself the stronger you are connected to other humans.

May a universal spirit touch you today, something that demonstrates to you that you are unique and yet connected.

Your gift today is rain.

Enso Morning

Now here is a new beginning. Today I got up early enough that no morning light had yet signaled the day's coming. This time of year courts darkness like an easy lover. At long last the windows lighten, the lovers part, and day begins.

As the room barely brightens, I sit in silence. Let the light bring the silence to you, through your skin and deep inside. Lighten your being with the calm of quiet…

Tune your remarkable body. Welcome your senses to the day so that they acknowledge your physical self, part by part and thus the whole: your feet steadying you, your legs and middle, your chest breathing you, and arms, neck and head, guiding you.

Bring your awareness to your emotional body, holder of your feelings. After a night of sleep, what feeling first appears on the empty plain? Again, use your senses to see, hear, touch, taste, even smell the coming feeling.

That ultimate sense intuition is the first messenger of spirit. Create some time to listen. Leave judgments and astonishment aside so the message gets through.

May you, this day, be open to receive messages. May you also carry and deliver messages.

Your gift today is a message.

Enso Morning

Here is a clean slate. Forget for a moment that you have anything planned for today, that you will eat your usual breakfast or that the day will meet your expectations. Walk this thin line between anxiety and excitement.

Explore this unknown territory in silence. Experience whatever shows up on your blank screen as a parade of events to witness. Here they come, there they go. Be a witness…

This morning after sleep, I felt myself arrive back into my body landing like a NASA Shuttle, some big bug miraculously navigating its way home from a deep journey. Welcome home.

Being grounded and having a home allow us to have our feelings. There is a sequence in play and feelings come along. And when feelings come, all else drops away as it should. What are you feeling right this moment?

At all these parades, a wise old lady sits on the curb watching, smiling at all the fuss and holding a flag with one hand and silently waving with the other hand: your spirit.

May you show up at your own parade today, appreciating what comes along. Allow yourself to be surprised.

Your gift today is showing up.

Greetings. How can you make the way smooth for yourself as you begin this day? Often we wait or manipulate, hoping others will give us what we need. See how you can begin this day at home, giving yourself what you need, right now.

Outside the dim gray world is heavy, silently pregnant. Bring silence inside and be pregnant with your own silence. Broaden, lengthen, and deepen this quiet time…

Feel your fullness. Inhabit every part of yourself so that you bring consciousness to your whole body: your feet on the floor, your legs, your knees, your waist, your chest, your arms, your head held aloft.

Knowing they were conceived in the past, years or minutes ago, give birth to your feelings. Feel the pain of creation, of being alive, and the relief of emptying out what is destined to be born.

Any act of creating has spiritual parents. This morning is creating itself around you. Let yourself experience the natural unfolding that is fueled by the spirit of creation, so ancient, so present and so inclusive of you.

Know that every breath you take and every step you make is a creative act. Join other creators today to craft a world of your own making.

Your gift today is to parent yourself.

Enso Morning

Welcome to the mystery of this day. The early darkness covers even familiar shapes and forms. My eyes think they know what is outside the windows and my mind wants to know, but right now there is no confirmation. There is only consciousness.

Be conscious of the background of silence that exists underneath everything. After the knock and hiss of the steam radiators that warm the morning house, silence returns. Bring the silence into the foreground and breathe it in, and out…

Stretch yourself as you continue to wake up. Use your mind to remember each part of your body, then actually stretch each part: toes, feet, legs, hips, chest, shoulders, neck, arms, head.

Reach, too, into your emotional self, on a voyage of discovery. Find out what you are already feeling. Bring back the precious feeling, value it, savor it, and when you are ready, let it go.

Sometimes, despite all our work and wishes, we simply don't know. This is a time to be with mystery and rely on what is unseen. Something is there that transcends both darkness and light, joining us with spirit.

May you today experience the spirit beyond having to know. May you find some comfort relaxing into the unknown.

Your gift today is mystery.

As you leave seamless sleep and join the texture of the morning, the day is glad to have you. Overnight a thin layer of new snow graces the ground, now decorated like sprinkled powered sugar on a plain cake.

Let white silence fall over you, bringing peace. Each snowflake drifts down independently yet is part of the blanket touching us with quiet and somehow with solace…

Allow yourself, your body, to be touched. Touch back with every part, even if it is only to meet the air around you. Touch with your feet and legs, your waist and chest, your arms and head.

How fleeting a feeling is when it has life and

expression, like a snowflake's brief existence, falling down through the sky and either melting away or blending into millions of its brothers and sisters, safely on the ground.

What is this quiet grace that the snow brings? Suddenly every object outside, bush, picnic table, sidewalk, and every person too, is stitched together by white; we are silently reminded of the invisible threads that join us all.

May you, too, remember today how alike we all are, even in our different forms; that while we follow different paths, we have a common destiny.

Your gift today is a snowflake.

Allow yourself to be welcomed to this day by your surroundings, both what you can see as well as what you can sense. All that is around you says, "Hello, how are you today?" and means it.

All this greeting happens in silence: the silence accomplishes all the communication, just as the wet earth and the puddles left from the rain are dried out without a sound and leave a deeper silence behind...

Feel yourself as a physical form with weight, height, and depth. Experience how your body holds you to the earth, all of you, your feet and legs, middle and chest, arms and head, one form held here.

Nothing so tangible holds your emotions. Let go

enough to feel feelings. What are the pools of feeling lying around? Some I have to jump in feet first and empty by splashing. Others I must let evaporate.

And in the air, all around, like close humidity, is spirit. Sometimes spirit feels moist, like a thick all-touching fog.

May you be touched this day by the moisture of life itself, the air and water combination that every seed requires to grow.

Your gift today is water.

Welcome to this day already in progress, a work of art in process, a big canvas with but a few brush strokes so far. I sit here, vacillating between an artist's ecstasy and despair saying in both cases, "Who, me?" The only answer is, as Mainers say, "Yup."

In between opposites, silence often lives. As we create silence now, the only noise is the soft rush of inhalation, then the soft sigh of exhalation. Notice the brief deep silence in between…

The one who breathes is the physical body. Let your breathing wake you up. Imagine your breath traveling down to your feet then back up bringing energy and life to your whole body, right now.

As you awaken your emotional self and begin to feel your feelings, notice that there is a space between your feelings created by having to take a breath. This space counts, too, as rest, and as the feeling of relief.

In between everything is spirit, the 'stuff' that touches us, that bonds us. When wounded, spirit shrinks. When healed, spirit expands. Be aware of when your spirit shrinks and when it expands.

May you today find and express the creative part of you. May you join all the other artists in your life creating this day.

Your gift today is artistry.

Another day, a day chock full of minutes, meetings and tasks, our units of measure. But allow yourself to be greeted by something much deeper than man-made markings. Open to the possibility that God, spirit, the life force, invites you to this day with no regard for what you do or accomplish.

In the early morning house the gloom gives up its darkness slowly and silently. In these silent moments, enormous transformations occur. What we will see when we open our eyes after quiet…

Notice how your clothes help you feel and outline your body. Physical touch is contact, and brings energy and awakens. Contact your physical self, each part, to remember a whole.

Sift down through to the pay dirt of your emotions. Mine the earth for gold. Even though you may not know the currency, remember the value of your feelings, the parts of your being seeking expression.

Deep down at the very core, surprisingly, is not solid rock but liquid spirit. Like water, spirit flows everywhere, even changing form, getting thick with mud or thin with air, and loves to join together and become a stream, a river, an ocean.

May you go deep this day, under man-made measures, to touch your core. Let the universal find expression in and through you.

Your gift today is depth.

Welcome. When I come downstairs this morning I remember when I sailed offshore climbing up on deck for my morning watch. I would leave the dark warm cabin below, and be surrounded by the sky. I would check the sail trim, then the navigation, and settle behind the steering wheel. Just like today.

There is so much silence, as big as the sky. We have nothing to do but join it, now. Yet it still feels like an act of creation, as we give birth to the quiet moments of our lives. Allow these calm moments their birth, one after another…

Come from the silence to your body, sitting here, your physical form. Scan who you are physically: touch with awareness your feet, your legs, your waist, your chest, your arms, your neck, and your head. Thus you create yourself anew.

Now you have the foundation for your feelings. Just as the water cradles a ship, so do your feelings cradle who you are. Let them emerge into this day without judgment, as naturally as breathing and as life giving.

Breath is spirit. As you breathe, your spirit lives. Breathing out, your spirit joins the world. Breathing in, your spirit is nourished by the world. Doing both, you are both nourished and nourishing.

May you come out into this day breathing and flourishing. May other flowers welcome your presence all day long.

Your gift today is to flourish.

Greetings. All the rehearsals for this day are over. Ready or not here it is. It is both a brand new beginning and a continuation. Much greets me today that is familiar, both around me and inside me. Still, the conductor's baton is in my hands: the symphony of this day begins.

In any piece of music the quiet times are just as necessary (and take just as much work to create) as the noisy notes. Join me in the quiet places right now. Create silence out of silence and let it exist...

You are the instrument, the maker of the music of your life. This body requires care, loving maintenance; give some now: focus and send love to each part: feet, legs, waist, chest, arms, neck, head.

After the rest of sleep, consciousness arrives slowly, sinking down into the depths to find, eventually, some emotion. A feeling is waking up, stirring, stirring you in its own process and progress toward expression.

So too with soul. The song of your soul hums along, usually in the background, your deep theme. Be your own musician today. Play your own song this day.

May you sing your way through the day, joining the other members of the orchestra. Listen to both ancient and new tunes.

Your gift today is music.

Welcome to the day. I come downstairs, still wearing the night's cloak, that warms me against the chill of the day. I leave the purity of sleep to find the purity of the new day.

Wear this fine but vanishing cloak of night in silence. Repeat the silence of night right here, only be awake. Let the silence continue with your present wakefulness...

Come to your body, where you live. Awaken your body with awareness, by seeing, actually or in your mind, every part. Starting with your feet, move upwards to your legs, bringing awareness. Then to your waist, now your chest. Include your fingers, arms, your head and hair.

Find your pure feelings. No artificial ingredients. What is it that you feel right now? Hold it in your awareness. Turn it over; investigate it as you might a shiny shell discovered on a beach walk. A feeling is a precious find.

Pure, shiny, fragile: such is spirit. Sometimes lost. Or imagined lost. Your spirit waits patiently to be discovered, recovered, and uncovered. Honor the process of spirit, its existence and its expression.

May you retain and regain what is pure in you this day, the core, the essence. Look for the essential ingredient in whatever and whomever you encounter today.

Your gift today is purity.

Here you are with the many people who make this transition from unconsciousness to consciousness. Remember that consciousness is cumulative; that what you learned yesterday is still inside you. This day is simply another school lesson.

Rattling radiators fade into the background as silence takes over now. Rattling thoughts come, and then they too drop away leaving only silence. Quiet comes, the quiet of not knowing what to say, and of not having to say anything...

Return to your body from the inside out, so that awareness grows like a seed flowering, stretching out to inhabit your whole physical frame. Keep stretching, and move so that you begin again to experience yourself a human form in the world.

Again from the inside, bring forth your emotions. Whatever feeling comes needs to come. Embrace it as you would a long-lost friend unexpectedly encountered on a street corner. Inquire what this friend would like to say. And listen.

These friends introduce you to deeper friends, those of the soul. This can be a crowded meeting, for like-minded souls are glad to hang out together, especially with all the barriers of time and space non-existent. Be not alone with your soul.

May you this day be friends with your deepest self, and find friends wherever you go.

Your gift today is to be a friend.

Good morning in the truest sense. Another major transition is so soon upon us, the meeting of night with day. I walk in a field of Christmas trees and tromp through mud that was once rain, then met the grass and earth, and made something entirely new.

The trimmed but un-chosen trees stretch over the rolling field. Each one stands erect, and points a bony finger silently to the light blue sky. How patient the trees are. Join the patience of trees now, and sit in silence with your mind open to the sky…

Remember it is your body that you inhabit first before anything else. Flesh yourself out, literally. Remind and rebuild your physical self for this day, starting with your feet, then legs, knees, waist, chest, arms and hands, and neck and head, a whole being.

Feelings are a mixture of elements, like soil and rain. Something has to come down, or up, and stir feelings. And something always will, as long as we are alive, wherein lies a clue: feelings bring life.

Then comes soul, stirred up by emotions. Usually shy, tender and fragile, not used to the limelight or any light, soul seeks only expression. How might you offer that today?

May you this day walk unafraid to stir things up a bit. Remember the elements often require the creative human touch, and we certainly need the elements; we need to get our hands into the mud.

Your gift today is a mixture.

Greetings. As new as this day is, some patterns repeat. Allow yourself to coast when you can. You don't have to cook a five-course meal in a stranger's kitchen every day. Enjoy the patterns of your life.

With a history of meditation, creating silence becomes easier. Each time is like coming back to familiar landscape. I know the pathway and remember the exhilaration of the view. Come back to your silence...

Familiarize yourself with your own body. Come to know your self again by breathing in, filling your lungs with air, thus sending energy throughout your whole system. Energize your feet, legs, waist, chest, arms and head.

Take the time now to search for feelings. Whether what you find is familiar or brand new, encourage what you find. If familiar, welcome a friend; if new, rejoice in the very newness.

Come back to the familiar parts of yourself at the deepest level and return to the familiar territory of soul, a landscape that has existed for centuries. Consider how you might inhabit this old territory in this new day.

May you walk into this day with sure steps, secure in the knowledge that you have traveled this way before.

Your gift today is familiarity.

Welcome. In the quiet of the very early morning, I hear the falling rain hit the roof and clatter in the gutter. The darkness makes the rain seem big, powerful, a force to be reckoned with, a reminder that the day already has a presence.

Find a way now to just let everything drop into silence, including your being. Let go; let silence happen as you simply sit here, simply breathing, in and out, in and out. Every breath is a silent raindrop, falling a thousand feet from the gray sky above...

Experience yourself breathe from the inside out. Let the fresh air come in and travel through your body, and wake your physical self. All your parts feel the breath of fresh air: your nose and mouth, throat and lungs, then down to your toes and back up again.

Imagine you are standing under a waterfall. The water pours down and washes your feelings out. The strong water is insistent, finds its way into all the hidden places, and scours out any feeling, cleaning and shining as it goes. Let your feelings pour from you.

What is uncovered can feel exposed and fragile. And it is; yet after all the layers have been washed away, something pure remains, some quality of essence, something that can be reduced no further. See how you might honor your essence today.

May you allow this day to wash over you, so that whatever is not necessary falls away, leaving you clean, freshened, and pure.

Your gift today is falling water.

Enso Morning

The day calls. The windows rattle and clink from the strong wind blowing outside. Even as light penetrates the gloom, everything is moving, swaying, rustling and creaking. This symphony beckons, bending its many crooked fingers at me, saying come, join the chorus of the day.

Now the noises fade into the background and the movement becomes silent and interior. Let all the distractions rush by, going on their merry way. Inhabit the vacuum they leave behind: feel the slowing down and the relief of this quiet time…

Slow way down so that you return to your home, your physical being. Stopped, you can be with yourself. Feel who you are physically. Feel your toes, feet, legs, knees, waist, belly, ribs, chest, arms, hands, neck, head, and hair. Here you are, all of you.

Reassured of a home base, what emotions move inside you right now? Notice the currents, gentle and fierce, that are alive and seeking expression. How natural it is to let both the strong winds and the gentle breezes blow, to let the winds of emotion blow through and be gone.

In this fresh quiet, spirit can emerge, asking, "Is it safe here?" Again reassured, spirit can speak. Listen carefully. This precious voice comes from the deepest place of the present.

May you hear the voices in the wind today, and include your own, joining the chorus, going with the flow, riding the currents.

Your gift today is wind.

Welcome to the day that has arrived. Nothing happens in the present without letting go of the past. The warm bed embraces and the bedclothes cling, but they must be cast off before a step is taken into the new day. We have to practice saying our goodbyes, over and over.

Let the chant of goodbyes fade into the distance so that the present brings silence. On a cold morning here, the silence is thin and brittle, like the new ice on the small pond by the edge of the woods. Even inside, my breath seems thin today, as it emerges, distinct from the past, new in the present…

Come again to your body, and ground yourself in the physical, your physical self. Breathe today's life into your body; breathe down into your toes, into your legs, into your middle, into your chest, into your arms, and finally into your head.

And now breathe life down into your feelings. The feeling relishes life and expression. The feeling, once expressed, loses its energy and the future beckons, and then becomes the present, available for another feeling.

Each moment of the present is an opportunity for soul to express. The way is prepared, the path is clear. But what will it require? What gift will lure the shy spirit forth? Simply the fertile ground of the prepared present.

May you not linger in the past today, but say your little goodbyes whenever necessary, and move into the present.

Your gift today is to let go.

Welcome. My senses are alert to the slow growth of light in this new day. Forms emerge out of the shadows. Hope is alive. Where there once was darkness now there is form and substance.

Many transformations occur in silence. Spread this silence out over seconds, then minutes, so that meditation is born. This quiet time stretches out around you, to bless you and keep you…

Feel the form and substance of your body. Right now you are receiving, taking time, soaking up silence, noticing your physical self: legs, knees, waist, chest, arms, head. All together a unique package.

Emotions need their own time, time to be, to be

acknowledged, to be felt and to be expressed. Offer your emotions this time now. Allow whatever the feeling is to come forth. It is yours.

The vacuum left by expressing feelings is not really an empty place. There is relief. And then spirit has room to breathe. Listen to the whisper of spirit and let it grow. A sigh or a scream: your spirit.

May you go into this day with hope, with the intention to live out your spirit.

Your gift today is hope.

Overnight the clouds vanished and this new morning is clean and clear. Welcome to the clarity of a fresh day, a fresh look. The sunshine itself is fresh and new, as if it is trying itself out for the first time, to see what it can illuminate.

The sun comes in silence, its rays splashing onto the street and houses, brightening the earth colors. Let silence shine on you now, cleaning and clearing as it comes. Silence does its work: cleaning up and clearing out the distractions…

Sitting here, it is the body that holds the five senses, that observes and experiences everything. Review and relish your physical self, even as it continues to serve you: your feet, legs, waist, chest, arms and head.

Let your attention illuminate your emotions, no matter what they are. Shine awareness on a feeling and energize it to expression, so that a word or sound comes out into the air right now, here.

Shine the light all the way down into your soul and illuminate your essence. This is you, and yours, and shines more brightly whenever it is shared.

May you shine today, illuminating who you are, and others in your light.

Your gift today is illumination.

Blessed be this day and you who are experiencing it. We emerge from the warm cocoon of sleep into the bright world of sensations. Open your eyes to really see, literally and figuratively, what your world is, and the added dimension of what your world can be.

As light spreads in silence, so can we see more and more. Encourage the silence to come, to stay and to deepen. Both light and silence grow and spread, grow and spread...

Here, sit and experience the day, with your body. How can you, at this moment, strengthen your ownership of the body that gives you a home on the earth? Visit each part right now: legs, knees, hips, waist, chest, arms, neck and head.

Now see what feelings you own. Without any need to categorize or understand, allow the feelings to lighten, to float to the surface and find expression, like an air bubble winding its way from great depth to free itself from the water and come into the light.

Free your spirit in the same manner. Let your spirit bubble up and overflow. Remember the delicious relief of discovering we are not alone. Let spirits mingle.

May your load lighten today. Drop what you no longer need, so your world brightens and lightens.

Your gift today is light.

In the gray early morning, the wide arms of the beach reach out to the ocean and embrace the gentle curve of water. In the same way, let the day embrace the part of you that is available at this beginning moment.

At the beach there is only the soft murmur of wavelets lapping up the sand, then back, like breath in meditation. Breathe like the waves: in and out, up and back, over and over, extending the ocean, returning to the ocean…

Feel your breath, the coolness coming in, and the soft rush going out. Breathe all the way in, sending fresh air from the universe to every part of your body: down to your feet, through your legs and torso, around your midsection, into your arms and back out your throat and mouth.

With this quiet new energy, search for signs of feeling; when you find them, amplify them. Breathe so that feelings have life and movement, and can move out to expression, right now, right here.

So too breathe life into your spirit. Like your breath, spirit is an expression of who you are at a most pure level. Spirit asks nothing but expression, requiring only that you recognize who you are.

May you enter this day both embraced and embracing.

Your gift today is an embrace.

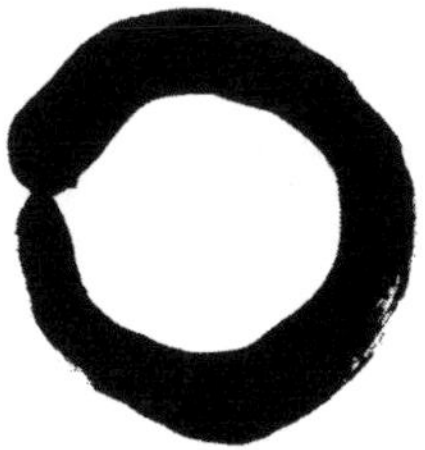

This is one of the new days in a new year; these markings are our attempt to measure and control nature. Outside in the lightening day the calm warm night has changed to a blustery day, cold and icy. How can we join the changes?

Even the wind quiets for moments at a time. Extend these moments into prolonged silence. Come inside and quiet the interior gales with your own natural breathing…

Be as a mountain with your body, solid, unmoving yet alive. Notice all your parts, from top to bottom, and back around: torso, limbs, bones deep, flesh on the surface, all you.

Let the changes affect what you are feeling. Only when you give life and expression to this feeling can the natural cycle of change continue. In this way you facilitate – make easy – the continuing expressions of your emotional life.

Under the winds of change lies your spirit, serene, gracious and patient. There is nothing you have to do, save honor it.

May you go into this day steady on your feet, joining the multitude of change happening inside and outside.

Your gift today is transformation.

Hello. Here is another day, more of life, today more of snow, too. A light white dusting covers everything outside. Gentle energy high in the sky created snowflakes, which fall lazily to our earth, gifts from the heavens.

The snow falls silently and lies quietly, content to make no sound. Find a similar place of contentment inside yourself and sit quietly. When distractions come, let them fall away, making no sound, leaving you in silence…

Gently bring your consciousness to your body. See what you can see of yourself, the exterior. Feel what you can feel, the interior. Bestow some appreciation on your physical being, from your feet upwards to your head.

Visit the places where you carry your emotions and let them go, one at a time. Let a feeling fall away from you by expressing it. As more come, continue letting them drop from you.

Some essence can be revealed. Some quality of spirit, unseen but real nonetheless, is uncovered. Offer this spirit of yours some time, and some place in your life, some manifestation, today.

May you keep what is essential today, and let the rest fall away.

Your gift today is quiet energy.

Enso Morning

Welcome. Walking my dog Zoey in the nearby woods, each new step I take crunches loudly down into the frozen snow-frosted leaves. No one has stepped in this exact path before. We are, like it or not, exploring virgin territory, every step, every day.

Now step into the landscape of silence, where you can hear your own heart beat. Listen for whatever is present, and no matter what you hear, keep listening. Listen anew each breath you take…

And listen to your body. Up from the cells come messages of health and healing, informing, instructing, and requesting. Offer each bone, each organ, and each muscle recognition and appreciation.

Emotions too arise from the cellular level. Explore what feelings make their way to consciousness right now. Again, listen to them, to their messages, and join their song.

And today, right now, as you clear the way, allow yourself to walk into the territory of spirit. Make one step at a time, create your own unique path as you go deeper into the woods, and make them your own territory.

May you find your path easy today, explorer that you are. Know that to walk your own path requires both direction and courage.

Your gift today is to explore.

This day begins, at whatever hour it is for you, and the day's time ticks, and beckons to you: come, see what is available. I clean old ash off my brass ship's clock, years after a fire, to reveal not just a shiny yellow surface, but a deeper, richer luster than before.

Layers of debris exist on everything, cloaking us in silence. Huddle now in this silence; use it for your own peace in these moments. Welcome the shelter that silence provides right now…

Every physical object, including our bodies, has layers and layers. Go down now, in your imagination, deeper into your layers. Feel beneath your own surface, your skin, and all the way down to your bones and marrow, bringing awareness, appreciation and energy.

With emotional layers, first come, first served. While there is no formula, no prescription, each layer deserves and will take its own time. Let the foremost feelings up, to live and to express, right at this moment, here.

Ephemeral, fleeting, spirit hovers like fog, or vanishes completely like mist in sunlight, or roars forth like an ancient animal god. How can you prepare the way for your spirit, with its many faces and many depths?

May you peel away the surface of the day today and discover depths.

Your gift today emerges layer by layer.

You are welcomed into this new day. Knowing that I am going to write every morning deepens my awareness and opens my consciousness. Passive receptivity grows into active exchange with the world around me. See how you can add yourself to the world right now.

Sitting here in this silence, breathe into the world's stillness. Let the silent moments come, as they stretch out, expanding the present. Be not passive but active, be not rest but an exploration...

Expand your awareness now into your body, exploring who you are physically at this moment. See and feel yourself anew, with new eyes and new feelings. Discover your feet, legs, waist, chest, arms, and head.

This is your physical self.

Instead of waiting for an emotion to surface, initiate a search, commission a journey to find a feeling. Be the active one. Take the step to actively encourage your feelings.

Something deep inside relaxes, relieved at giving up the protection. Soul is exposed. You have summoned up from the depths some of your essence, some of your core. Feel the freedom of being who you are.

May you go into this day actively; put energy into your life, receive energy from your life.

Your gift today is activity.

Enso Morning

The house wakes up slowly, just like me. First a light here, while the outside world is dark, then some warmth there, as the radiators clank and hiss. Welcome to your waking up, no matter the time of day.

As there is more light to see on the outside, light that illuminates gray corners, let silence shine inside, melting away distractions. When gloom fades, what is it that you are able to perceive?

Sitting here, wake up your physical self, part by part, so that you make connections with how you think of your body: these are your feet grounding you, and your legs, your waist, your chest, your arms, and your head, each doing their part.

And somewhere inside live your emotions. Where do you feel your feelings? From what depth do they come? What matters, of course, is that they do come, that they have some pathway up and out, some avenue of expression. Do what you can to open the way.

Opening, cobwebs fall away, and we enter a new territory, and we perceive ourselves differently, so that we in fact are different. We are more ourselves when we let our insides show, for our essence is exposed and our being is out.

May you this day see yourself with fresh eyes. As you see yourself differently so will your world be different.

Your gift today is perception.

Begin again. Start over, again. Newness and sameness. When I come downstairs, my feet step down on each stair tread in the same spot as yesterday. I duck my head at the same low point just at the right time, as always. Yet it is today, not yesterday and it is now, not then.

I come down into the silence of the night, which now changes slowly into the silence of the day. Silence is the bridge. Walk across this long bridge right now, taking your time and enjoying the view…

Come back gently to your body and remind yourself of your physical presence. Scan your body, sending awareness and energy as you go: feet, legs, thighs, waist, chest, arms, neck, head and face.

In the same way check to see what emotions are starting to stir, are beginning to rustle and rumble around. Let a feeling start to come, to rise to consciousness. Once in the mind, move it to your mouth and say the words out loud, into the air.

After worldly concerns, it is relief to relax down into the ever-present realm of spirit, like falling onto a soft, comfortable sofa after a long day. Feel the familiar support and loving cradling of your spirit that welcomes you.

May you find not only one, but multiple new ways to begin today.

Your gift today is to begin.

You are graced with this new day, all the firsts, seconds, minutes, and hours that stretch out in front of you. As I was lying in bed, beginning to awaken, I made no effort to bring the day. There was nothing to do; the day, like much in our lives, comes by itself.

Let silence come now. It really is already here. All we have to do is stop doing, so that we can notice, appreciate and enjoy the stillness. The silence spreads out like a warm mirror, constantly reflecting us back to ourselves...

Turn attention and therefore energy to your body just now. Reflect back your image so that you nurture yourself without effort. It is you who can take care of yourself, by giving energy to each part, from your toes all the way up to the top of your head.

Move gently to your emotions, which are already there, here. Feelings do not have to be created; they exist because we are alive and human. They ask the breath of life, which we give them naturally.

And now breathe down into your spirit. Remind yourself of who you are. Again, there is nothing to do, except be yourself, effortlessly.

May you continue this day as the best expression of yourself, the unique person that you are.

Your gift today is mirrors.

Here comes the day, the time, and the opportunities. As I walk around the house, I feel my feet hit the floor and I appreciate the force that keeps me here on the earth. I can count on gravity.

This force, though not always its consequences, works in silence. Let the pull of the earth ease you into stillness. Allow gravity to hold you to your home, binding you to the still place you occupy…

It is your physical body that the earth pulls close and claims. The same force that controls that spinning of the planets helps keep your feet on the ground, helps keep you grounded.

It feels sometimes as if emotions are held too close,

buried. But they have no real mass, and can float to the surface, like a bubble of air coming up from a great dark depth. Breathe fresh air into your feelings so they can float.

Also in the depths of your being lives your soul. The black depths seethe and roil in their own agony of birth, and black goo clings to what emerges into the light, providing a humble reminder of our humanity.

May you come into this day with appreciation for all the forces that keep you on the earth and on your own particular path.

Your gift today is gravity.

Welcome. The great black elm, oak and maple tree branches arch over the street outside, reaching their scraggly arms, thinner and thinner, dark against the lightening sky. A kind of cathedral is created, two-toned, completely open, welcoming.

The trees stand in front of the sky in magnificent stillness. No wind harvests their sounds in the morning quiet. Take the offered silent time for your own. Be like a tall tree, connected with the earth below and reaching into the sky above...

Feel your feet on the floor, which is connected to the earth below you, and feel the earth's solidity and energy move up through your legs. Into your middle it comes, to your chest. The charge moves out your arms, and up your neck to your head, energizing.

The pulse of life finds feelings. Some are familiar. Oh, this again! Some are brand new. What is this? Old or new, these are your feelings. They poke their heads up like prairie dogs, to sniff at the light of the new day.

And underneath your feelings, and related, are your spirits, sometimes shy, sometimes raucous. They too emerge, and they too connect the depths with the heights.

May you enter today with an appreciation for your range, the distance you can cover.

Your gift today is contrast.

As the earth turns, it brings the horizon of a new day, to our sky and to our doorstep. The sky is a sweet deep blue overhead, and melts gently down to the pale, promising horizon in the east. So the day comes to us.

Yet again this momentous change, the biggest transformation of all, that from darkness to light, occurs in silence. Let this same powerful silence come to you at this moment. Extend your silent moments here in this present…

Tune in to your body. Listen for its healing messages. Hear what parts are requesting attention and nurturing, what scratches, itches, aches and pains are seeking energy, a touch, a massage, a loving thought or caress. Offer what you can, from the bottom of your feet up to the top of your head.

In the same fashion, listen to your feelings. Discover what your emotional body is asking for. First, it wants to be heard. Maybe that's all, enough for now. Perhaps, though, this feeling would like to be named, to be touched, to be taken out for a walk, to see the light in the sky, to see the horizon.

The day's light is available for your spirit, too. After the heaviness and mystery of the darkness, here is the freedom and space your spirit seeks.

May you see the light that is shining on your path today.

Your gift today is fresh horizons.

Welcome to this morning. We go from horizontal to vertical, from dark to light, from unconsciousness to consciousness. Outside, the dark tree branches stand out against the light sky in the background, each emphasized by the contrast.

Silence has age about it. Tap into old silence, the stillness that comes from long ago, the quiet that exists when we don't know what to say, but are willing to be present, to sit and witness...

Search your body and find your physical self, here all the time, providing you with form and substance, a toolbox we often take for granted, at least until suddenly one of the tools gets rusty or won't work properly. Offer appreciation and energy to each part of your physical being.

Emotions are tools, too, the tools of relationship: self to self, and self to others. Rummage around and see what you find at this fresh moment. What feeling is ready to be picked up and put to work, to help repair something or create something new?

The background that shows the foreground is spirit. As spirit informs and inspires us, spirit shows us who we are and how to be ourselves; indeed how to just be.

May you experience this day everything in your foreground, in the context of your spirit, who you have always been.

Your gift today is your toolbox.

Brilliant crystals of frost cover the windows this cold morning, back lit by the low rising sunlight. Such a display demands attention, saying, "Here, look at this!" The window, in keeping the cold out, transforms its function into a work of art.

In total silence, the window marks the boundary between the cold outside and the warmth inside. The stillness is neither cold nor warm, just stillness. Let the quiet be a window into yourself...

View your body and come inside to experience your physical self, sitting here, breathing, and living. Your vision passes through your skin and travels around your body, waking and energizing every part.

Underneath another kind of skin lie your emotions. You can melt this boundary enough to allow the passage of feelings, whatever they may be. The light and warmth pass through to bring life to your emotions.

Needing the protection of our skins, our essence lives inside, inhabiting our core. Find a way to reach across, reach down and touch that quality of essence, with care and respect, but also with appreciation and energy.

May you both respect and transcend boundaries this day.

Your gift today is windows.

Welcome. The fresh frost carves curves of lacy designs onto the windows, turning ordinary panes of glass into holy artwork. Morning light is crystallized and fills the east-facing rooms with gentle splendor.

All this in silence. And even as the light shimmers and grows, there is no sound to break these magic moments. Join your inner light to these still moments. Let the merged lights grow in silence...

Look and feel inside your surface, and discover anew your physical being: from your feet to your legs, from your waist to your chest, from your arms to your hands, and from your neck to your head.

Every windowpane begins as empty glass, before

anything is seen on it or through it. When we take the time to look, a feeling often emerges out of nothing; a feeling crystallizes and expresses itself, as it does now.

Just as beautiful crystal grows in fertile conditions, so does soul flourish with space and reflection. Soul can be a place for the light of the universe to land, to adhere to, to warm and beautify. Welcome the light available.

May you collect the light streaming toward you today.

Your gift today is crystal.

Welcome. Thick, gray, ancient-looking sea ice clings to the tops of certain rocks like old men's beards lying in the sun at the wrong time of the year, as if they had been caught sleeping in church. The low winter sun shines on this spectacle, and warms me to astonishment.

Even the powerful opposites ice and sun exist in silence on the wide flat beach. Let your opposites coexist in these wide moments of silence, so that nothing disturbs your peace; your earth and sky are one...

Feel your body as its solid parts support the soft parts, and the soft parts hold the solid parts. Circulate your awareness from your feet on the floor up through your whole physical system, admiring and appreciating.

To live life we need the full range of feelings, rage and tenderness, sorrow and ecstasy, despair and hope. Take this time to allow, to encourage and to welcome whatever feeling waits in the wings like a talented but shy actress.

The gray rocks on the winter beach remind us of our true nature: the strength, the age, the solid wisdom, and the link with the stars. We are the rocks, the beach and the stars.

May you today drop your limits and fill in the extremes so that the full range of yourself is available to you.

Your gift today is opposites.

Allow yourself to be welcomed by the spreading light. Here, the snow cover amplifies the dim morning light so that it comes not only from the brightening sky but upwards from the earth itself: the rock and dirt have their own kind of light to contribute.

Move out of your own kind of darkness into the light of silence. Imagine this silent light growing inside you, shining into all the shadowy corners, bringing the gift of stillness, absolute quiet…

In such silence we may not even notice our body. Move a tiny piece of your awareness to your physical being; sit here being still. Your breath comes in and goes out. The spark of life moves through your whole body.

Let the spark ignite a feeling. Whether it glows gently like a candle or roars like an inferno, feel the warmth and life of a feeling coming to life. Soak up the heat and health of a feeling coming alive.

To express emotions warms the soul, and burns a pathway down to essence. Under the flames and soot is a soul that awaits discovery.

May you fan the flames of your life today.

Your gift today is melting.

Welcome to this new day, here at last. Consider how much inertia this day has, how it is simply another day in the endless succession of days. The sights and sounds that now herald its beginning have such a stellar history, a history that, right now, you are joining.

Powerful as the past is, it exists only in our silent memory. Bring the silence of the ages into this present moment, so that it covers you in a cloak, woven of threads made from intimacy and love...

Imagine all the people who have paused, like you do now, to sit and become more in touch with themselves. Remember how much in common we all have: our legs and arms to move us through the world, our waist and middle holding our organs, our head with our brains and senses.

The link with our ancestors is emotional, too. You join so many when you feel love, resentment and sadness. Feelings belong to us all. It is not only your love, your resentment, your sadness, but also our love, our resentment and our sadness. And so does loneliness turn into community.

Even more so does spirit connect and protect us. Across time and space, spirit moves, inspires and directs us, if only we will give it time and space. Today offer these simple gifts to your spirit.

May you feel a part of life today, one of many.

Your gift today is history.

The round full moon and some smaller planets hang in the western sky, then, pulled by forces beyond comprehension, slowly slip behind a wispy white cloud. Join the pull of the planets as they take their places for another day.

In your own small orbit, find and settle into a place of silence. Let the universe spin on its own while you stay still, still and serene in your quiet place…

What is it that sits here, so still, but your physical being? Your legs the broad base, your trunk the solid core, and your head above.

You are a ball of feelings, pockmarked and cratered by hits. Yet still the sunlight reflects you perfectly.

And thus the pathway opens for spirit. Not stuck like a rigid religion, but alive and shining, your spirituality now finds a way to beam out.

May you be both powerful and serene this day.

Your gift today is the planets.

Enso Morning

In the western sky, the yellow-orange full moon was saying goodbye, slipping into clouds on the horizon, as the sun brought daylight in the east. For a moment, light from two planets. Welcome to the continuation of life's cycle.

Circle around to a natural silence, a time to quiet down, smooth out the wrinkles and coast into a silent meditation. Time to breathe in, breathe out, time for you, time for quiet…

Gently come back to your body. Notice who you are as a physical being. As you bring your awareness, so you bring your energy to each part of your body: toes, feet, legs, thighs, hips, waist, stomach, chest, arms, hands, neck, head, and face.

Circle deeper still, down into your emotions. Stir up from the bottom, like a good cook, so that all the ingredients, especially the spices, are included in the mix, and you have all your feelings available.

Spiral down to your essence, where something precious lives: your essential self, your spirit. Both fragile and strong, your spirit stirs, is awakened, and expresses.

May you cycle through the day, rolling along, coasting when you can.

Your gift today is a cycle.

Enso Morning

The world invites you to join this day. Even the deep winter black sky slowly dissolves now into a rich purple dawn, veined by the still dark tree branches. The reaching branches beckon.

Let yourself reach back into the silence of the night just past and pull a blanket of stillness over you. Feel the silence enter through your pores and melt down into your interior. Peaceful alertness. Alert peacefulness…

Later now, gently wake yourself up from the inside out. Warm up, bringing the glow of energy out to your whole body: your shoulders, chest, belly, then out to your legs, feet, and arms and hands, all the way to your toes and fingertips.

And so too, wake up your emotional self, so that you have access to your feelings, or more accurately, so that they have access to you. Let a feeling reach your consciousness, welcome it by giving it a name, and help it on its way.

In the aftermath of a feeling just expressed, there is a kind of vacuum, a fertile space. Do not be quick to fill it up, for emptiness has its own reward. Your spirit inhabits all your space without filling it up.

May you stride into and through this day filled with peace and spirit.

Your gift today is to reach.

Fall and flow into this day like a quiet cloud, whose moisture falls to the earth, becomes a stream, then a river, and eventually joins the vast ocean. What we used to be changes into what we are.

Even the quality of silence changes. As I sit here meditating in the retreat center, the silence deepens and deepens, pulling out of the old woodwork the ancient silences of priests long gone, except for their faded photographs lining the still stone hallways…

I am reminded that I still have my body, or more rightly said, my body still has me. Sometimes, of course, it's hard to have a body, this body. But here it is and here I am. Revisit your familiar body, toes up to hair, to bring fresh energy for this new day.

While the seeds of all emotions are within us, the fruits, given manure, water, and sun, flourish only in their own time. Offer these ingredients to your emotions and enjoy the harvest.

With the celebrations and excitement of harvest time, we sometimes forget our deeper arches and hallways where spirits roam. Extend a hand to your spirit, which may be familiar, yet lonely at the same time. We must be spiritual friends to ourselves before we can be spiritual friends to others.

May the hallways of this day echo with the greetings of spirits in communion with each other.

Your gift today is fruition.

Welcome to another day full of opportunities to minister, to yourself and to others. Gentle slaps of rain hit the windowpanes. All the world feels wet as the water runs down the street, then underground and eventually finds it own way to the bay beyond.

These wet noises come and then go. When the sounds stop I am propelled off the cliff of the noise into a dry free flight of deep silence that is at once the absence of noise and the presence of a wider, deeper, fuller expanse of silence…

Such unique combinations of wet and dry, our bodies combine the elements to give us life as humans. Feel your heart pump your blood throughout your whole body, rhythmically and regularly, bringing nutrition to every far part.

And how far must you travel to bring solace and life to your emotional regions? Bringing care and energy to your feelings, you can then offer expression. First is surviving, and then comes thriving. And to thrive, we express our feelings, somehow, some way, and somewhere.

Ask yourself what your soul requires. If you could give voice to your innermost being, what is it that he/she would most benefit from right now, how would your soul like to be ministered to today?

May you understand more today about your purpose here.

Your gift today is your ministry.

Welcome. I look up into the sky, and I see extraordinary clouds at the edge of a weather front moving through. Sharp northwest winds tear at the edge of the cloudbank, and rip off swirling, curling white streamers. The long shapes continually move, change and rearrange into new smaller clouds.

Even as the clouds roil and toil in the sky, no sound comes down to this earthbound watcher. Instead, silence reigns. Spread the quiet around you, lightly and gently, so that you are bathed in sweet serenity for these moments of your life…

Come slowly back into your body and notice what calls for attention and energy. Imagine a healing hand moving slowly up from your toes, to your feet and legs, bringing warmth and energy, which continues to your waist and chest, then finishes with your arms, neck and head.

As changing as cloud formations in a sky wind, feelings can only be caught in a brief moment of time, and then released. Any attempt to hold on, no matter how hard you might grasp, is only wasted effort: each feeling slides free, making room for the next one.

The immense sky behind the clouds is like the spirit behind the comings and goings of everyday life. Each needs the other to appreciate the magnificence in the ordinary.

May you find yourself moving with the breeze when it blows today.

Your gift today is clouds.

Already this day is unique and not quite like any other day that has ever been. Let yourself join this special day. White sea smoke covers the still harbor surface, alive and drifting, giving the illusion of widespread fire when in reality its source is not fire, but ice.

This sea smoke is to be the planet's own breath, escaping in complete white silence out into the frigid air. Breathe in silence yourself. Join your inner air with that around you, and take in the colder, newer breath of life...

Breathe from the inside out, so that you empty completely. Then bring the new air in to every part of your body, starting with your toes way down on the floor, and then around your whole system, bringing fresh air and energy for this new day.

Find the spark and fan the flames. See what fires burn within, what feelings smolder, looking for a way out. Tend and encourage the truth of your feelings: the flames of passion, the burn of sadness, the heat of anger, and the warmth of love.

Purified by our everyday conflagrations, large and small, lies spirit. Impervious to fire and ice, spirit waits patiently for fresh air, for the day's new opportunities.

May you tend your fires this day.

Your gift today is your spark.

The deep cold pushes heating systems to work hard, and houses pour thin streams of white smoke from their brick chimneys, as if to signal, "Here is a warm place." Let yourself be welcomed into the warm places of this day, wherever they may be.

The warmth of silence seeps into you like the radiant heat from a wood stove. Absorb the qualities of silence, the depth and stillness that allow you to drop down into yourself, even into regions that are yet to be explored...

Feel the gentle warmth produced by your own body and how it sends encouragement for life to every part of you: your toes and feet, your legs and thighs, your waist and midsection, your chest and arms, your hands and fingers, your neck and head.

Let the heat melt and loosen your emotions so that they liquefy and move around. Welcome the flow and see what floats on top. Ignore the content. It will always be something. Celebrate the process. Keep it moving.

In the molten core of life runs your spirit, powerfully affecting the course of every day, every moment. Feel your spirit simmering under the surface.

May you find the warm places and people in your life today.

Your gift today is warmth.

The whole harbor lies waiting as I walk down to the shore first thing in the morning. First breezes stir the surface into marching wavelets, except in the lee of the old stone pier. Here, resting behind the protective arm of the pier, the water stays still and dark.

You too can rest under a sheltering arm, right now. Accept and enjoy the silence offered. Be as calm water, with a smooth surface, but having depth as well. Let the stillness sink deeper…

Your body is the container for all the stillness, a whole harbor full. Feel your physical self stretch to hold all the quiet, your muscles expanding and contracting, even as you simply sit here noticing your body, both surface and deep within.

Just as with any body of water, there is both surface and depth to feelings. And there is movement: the tides and currents. Some feelings skim lightly along the surface while others stir ponderously the dark depths. Stir your feelings.

Welcome all the momentary protections, when they come, so that spirit has, like the harbor, places of calm. Imagine all the other moments of respite, in all the harbors of the world, and join this protected place, where spirit can reign.

May you today both find and offer arms that protect.

Your gift today is shelter.

Join with this, your day of days. I walk along the beach, and I notice the many brown stalks of marsh grass, sticking up six or seven inches from the sand, absolutely straight. Like the winter mooring sticks out in the harbor, they hold places all winter, waiting until the spring blooming.

All the sticks stand erect and silent in the cold morning air, sentinels of stillness. Sit straight yourself, so that you call the silence to you. Let the stillness wrap itself around your figure sitting here, like so many other people around the world...

Your body is like a reed coming up from the earth itself into the thin air of the day, a physical presence breaking into the vast sky. Feel your form existing in the soup of the universe, all of you: your legs and arms, your middle and chest, your head and face.

Ask yourself what feelings stand waiting patiently. Perhaps they hibernate until a warmer wind bids them welcome, and it is safe for them to bloom. Can they, will they, really wait? Breathe your own warm wind of acceptance on to your waiting feelings.

And holding everything, informing everything, is spirit, breath of life. Lord of both hibernation and blooming, spirit is everywhere all at once. Sleeping or waking, your spirit is uniquely you.

Even in this short day, may you find moments of rest.

Your gift today is hibernation.

Welcome. The frozen footprints in the forest speak of past walkers. Some of the prints could be mine from yesterday, reminders of a past path, showing the way if I choose to repeat myself, or showing how to avoid repetition if I choose a new course.

The footprint tells its tale in frozen silence, containing the mark of its owner's boot, and other stories to a talented sleuth. Let your stories lie frozen in the past, where they belong, and let yourself have this freeze frame in the present, to pause here, and be still...

Our bodies are accumulations of the past, which carry us into the present. Bring your physical being all the way into this time by noticing who you are physically: your feet and legs, your thighs and waist, your chest and neck, your arms and hands, your head and face.

Of all the feelings you have ever felt, what remains in the tiny slice of this present moment? It is here only because, like a footprint from the past, it has a story to tell. Listen. The feelings could be finished, continuing, or just beginning.

Continue to listen, at a deeper level, so that the story of your soul can be heard above the chatter of everyday life. Listen hard; listen well, for no tale is more precious to you.

May you go forth into this day to create the story you someday will be glad to listen to.

Your gift today is your story.

Bring yourself into this day that waits patiently, like a pair of familiar, well-worn boots. Far beyond the stiffness of being new, they are worn and formed to the shapes of your feet, like old friends knowing you intimately. The boots sit waiting, ready when you are to carry you into the day.

While most waiting is silent, the task is to be silent without waiting. Let yourself live simply and only for this silence, without any expectations. Fill out the moment so that this time, moment to moment, is enough. Enough. Sufficient. Right now...

Now come back to your body, where you have always been. Offer consciousness, that bright spark of energy, to your physical self, each and every part.

Now bring the same light of awareness to your emotional body, where your feelings live. No judgments about which feeling it is, just value whatever you find, be it anger, relief, joy, sadness, contentment. Remember that each and every feeling, given expression, will change.

Underneath, your spirit is both familiar and intimate. Precious, sometimes needing protection, spirit is the quality of you-ness that is constant, always known to you, if you will honor it.

May you remind yourself today of all that you know.

Your gift today is intimacy.

Above, the sky is bright baby blue, while the warm sun melts the ice from the high tree branches, creating thin, sparkling, bright columns of falling rain enclosed within the forest, a shining silver cathedral. The sounds of the drops finally touching the ground are sacred; the occasional tiny splashes anointments.

Let the small background noises fade farther behind you, so that the entire foreground is consumed with silence and you yourself are consumed by the stillness of the present. Let yourself be swallowed up by the silence.

Touch home base by re-membering your body now, bringing back consciousness to each and every part and therefore recreating your whole physical being:

feet, legs, middle, chest, arms, neck, head. Re-experience your own cathedral.

In the holy houses of our lives, feelings dwell. Given the safety of a home, emotions settle in, grow, and eventually leave like awkward kids, suddenly out there for the world to see and hear.

And in this very air floats our spirit, what we live and breathe, the cloud-like essence of ourselves that follows us everywhere because it is what gives us life itself.

May you carry your own cathedral with you today, light, bright, and full of your spirit.

Your gift today is your holy house.

My own little cloud of breath hangs briefly in the frigid morning air, and then is gone. Another breath, another disappearance. Yet I am still here for another day.

The wispy gray cloud of breath, so fleeting, exists and vanishes in silence so quickly one might ask, did it really happen? Was it really there? Breath, like silence, leaves no evidence. Trust your own silence not to require any monument, but simply, in this moment, to exist for its own sake…

Come home to the engine that produced the breath. Feel your lungs expand and contract, as they take in fresh air from the universe, send it throughout your body, then expel it back out from whence it came. No need to think about it, the process is built-in; it happens day and night, here and now.

Emotions, like breath, come and go, and often leave no sign behind. As natural and necessary as breathing, our anger, sadness, joy, grief, astonishment flare up and out into the present moment, then die away to nothing, leaving room, with the next breath, for the next feeling.

And under this cycle lies the spirit, a compassionate witness, sometimes a laughing companion, reminding us of who we are, remembering us as a dear family member, one of our own.

May you require no evidence of your life today except life itself.

Your gift today is to be invisible.

Enso Morning

Welcome to this day. My dog Zoey comes in the room, over to where I sit, and lies down firmly up against my leg. I didn't call her, she didn't ask permission, she just came. Her black and white body is now stretched out on the rug, content.

Zoey came in without noise. Let silence come in and lie at your feet, warming you with its presence. Feel the acceptance and companionship of the quiet world. Thoughts come, thoughts go, and always you have yourself…

Sitting here, come back to your body so that you come into your body. Quietly notice the parts of your physical being: your toes and feet on the floor, your legs and knees supporting you, your midsection holding your organs, your chest with your heart and lungs, and your head with your face.

Now notice what emotion comes in, to rub up against your consciousness, quietly announcing its presence. Perhaps the feeling doesn't require anything except to be your quiet companion, stretched out at your feet.

Your spirit is already present, hovering around, noticeable if not tangible, pervasive if not demanding. You are, of course, not so much someone with a spirit, as someone who is spirit. Remember and imagine how noticeable and pervasive you are as spirit.

May you find this day accepting of who you are.

Your gift today is acceptance.

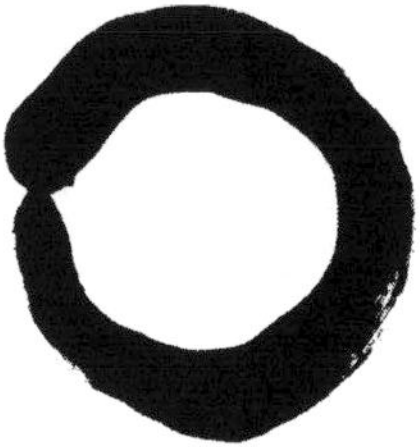

Lots of skin leaves the bed and encounters the fresh air of the new day. Our physical boundaries sense and feel how to use the world around us. Open up your pores to the day.

Take in the silence of the world, all the spaces between tumult and noise. Breathe these quiet moments until they are yours, your very being. With this silence comes the potential of the unknown...

With every breath, allow the world to bring fresh new energy. Let the air and energy enter and circulate throughout your whole physical system: down to your toes, then back up through your legs, waist, chest and head, and out your arms to your fingertips.

A feeling comes to the surface of your being, like an air bubble popping its fragile envelope and releasing its tiny air into the small sky above the pond. As much as we own our feelings, and sometimes feel as if they own us, our feelings really belong to the world.

So too, spirit, especially spirit, crosses thresholds to link us with the rest of the universe, even with the past and the future. And when we understand this and accept this, spirit links us to ourselves.

May you encounter this day with all of your surfaces.

Your gift today is skin.

In the gray sky and spread snow of the early dawn, a faint smell of the earth comes from some deeper place, reminding us of changes to come. Even with months of winter to go, light comes a little earlier and stays a little later, changing how the air feels.

Before the glare of the day, or some other distraction, use this time to move inward, to be with yourself. Let all else drop away: all needs, all musts, all shoulds. Free yourself to be a dear companion to your self…

Gently return your consciousness to your physical body, so that you fill yourself out with awareness. Find all parts of your physical being: toes, feet, legs, knees, thighs, waist, chest, arms, elbows, hands, fingers, neck, head and face.

Take a similar wake-up tour through your emotional body; look in the musty corners and dim attics, those ancient places most in need of the light of truth. No judgments about what you find. Awareness, then expression.

After all of this, there comes a moment of recognition, a moment of some constant, underneath everything. Your spirit is there, here, pervading and infusing everything. Indeed, spirit is not only in everything, but everything is spirit.

May you slow enough this day to absorb the subtleties around you.

Your gift today is your sense of smell.

Come into these moments of the day by joining life's process; life is underway. I listen to the jingle of my dog's collar as she investigates who is still in bed so she can join them; someone comes downstairs, stepping on the one stair tread that gives off a distinctive creak.

Now there is silence, outside and inside. The outside world recedes, drops away, back into the background. Here inside, in the foreground, is stillness, the calm of contemplation, when we look inside and see with new eyes who we are in this moment...

Fine-tune your ears to listen to the messages your body is giving you. Hear what part needs to be scratched, what part calls for a caress, or for a kind thought, and on and on, throughout your whole system.

And listen for your feelings as they whisper to you. You might hear a sigh of sadness, or a growl of anger, or a pant of passion, or a yelp of surprise, or a groan of despair, or a murmur of love. Listen, listen, listen.

While spirit may manifest through any of the five senses, it is part of the sixth and more quiet sense, intuition. Therefore, spirit asks for a certain kind of invitation, a gentle, unrushed availability. Consider how you might offer your spirit an invitation today.

May you hear with welcoming ears today.

Your gift today is to listen.

Piles of puffy, colored clouds, woven together in different shades of pink and orange, crowd the far horizon, and stretch toward me layer by layer. The citizens of the clouds have built their fleeting sky cities before me. Welcome to the textures of this new day.

Even at this great distance I can see the fiery forms changing and shifting, all in complete silence. Let heavenly silence descend on you, surround you and offer a brief respite from all your noise. Breathe in the quiet air, bring it inside you and pass it throughout your whole being…

Feel the fresh air come in, slightly cool, and travel to every part of you: your toes and feet, your legs and thighs, your waist and chest, your arms and hands and fingers, and your neck and head. You wake up layer by layer.

Under the physical, yet part of it, is the emotional. Look for the loose thread, the feeling out of place, waving in the wind, wanting attention. Notice its color and shape and texture, so that you can pull it out or weave it back into the fabric of your life, whichever it needs.

Underneath all the weavings is the loom itself, your spirit. See how your spirit directs the color, design and expression of who you are, living this life of yours. Find ways to enjoy this garment you wear.

May you appreciate extremes today.

Your gift today is texture.

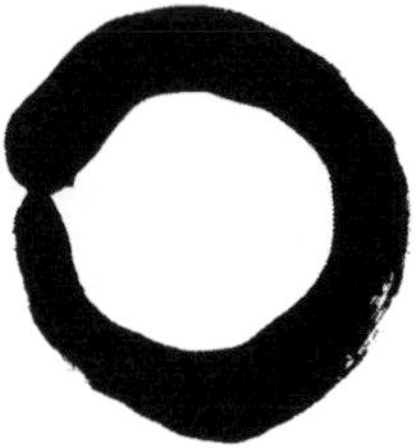

The day opens up clear and cold. It shows the islands across the wide bay as low blue-gray shadows sunken partly behind the curve of the earth. The new sunlight frosts the tops of every island near and far in a glinting glaze of light.

The frozen distances are made greater by the silence that stretches between here and there. The silence sinks down with the cold, invading every pore and closing off any sound so that everything freezes into stillness…

Even with so little motion, the body lives and breathes, home to consciousness on this planet. Travel the distances around your body, spanning the spaces with awareness: feet to legs, waist to chest, shoulders to arms, neck to your head.

How far is the distance to a feeling? Consider what it will take to bring a feeling closer. Sometimes all a feeling needs is a brief pause in all the busy-ness, a slice out of time, a timeless moment when all else drops away and only the sigh of the feeling exists.

Then the ordinary is revealed for what it is: both ordinary and extraordinary, the objects and the space in between where spirit does its work.

May you appreciate the distances you travel today.

Your gift today is your view.

Black crows caw their raucous welcome, caring not what they disturb. Their deep black shapes show only when they flap awkwardly away from the dark winter trees hiding them, in search of entertainment.

Crows gone somewhere, the trees suddenly silent, as if boisterous children have grown up and moved away. Keep this silence for your own, for at least these precious few minutes: no telling when the trees will attract new noisemakers. Quiet for now...

Feel physically how your body is like a tree, feet planted on the earth, a trunk to hold you solid and erect, arms like branches reaching into the sky, sometimes to the very heavens.

Feelings run through you like sap in the early spring, vital, but unseen much of the time, yet suddenly there, flowing from any sharp wound. And in the flowing out comes the healing, and the opportunity for new growth.

Deeper still flows the spirit, always there, here, acknowledged or not. No body, no time, no distance can contain spirit: feel how connected you are to those you love and who love you.

May your spirit flow today.

Your gift today is trees.

Underneath the sharp chill of the early morning breeze is a subtle and gentler taste, a tease of warmer winds and softer sighs. It is just a hint, but welcome enough, tantalizing evidence of winter's inevitable loss.

Even the momentous changes of the season begin in silence and end in silence. Come back to this silence from which we all come, and to which we will all return. Bring it now as both friend and reminder…

Flex and move and feel from the inside out your physical being. Move into yourself by joining consciousness with muscle, awareness with bone, energy with blood.

Continue the whole-making process by bringing

movement to your feelings. Let go of the content and encourage the process. Find the feelings underneath and tease them out.

The gentle breeze of your spirit blows through your life, never more so than today, right now. It brings both the taste of antiquity and the flavor of the present.

May you catch the scent in the wind today.

Your gift today is taste.

Enso Morning

Welcome. As I walk the morning beach, strong surf surges in under the fog, and boils to my feet. There is no sky and no sea, only fog. The curling waves march in, fiercely birthed by the fog itself, rush splashing at the steep stoned beach, then fall back noisily.

After this retreat a quiet moment comes over the beach. The waves are flat, but still move gently under the fog. Notice the silence between the waves of your breath. Feel the rush, then the quiet. Extend the silence a little more each time…

Breathe into your body to bring awareness, energy and peace to all parts. Send your breath not only into your lungs, but also from there down into your belly, waist, legs and feet. And bring the wave back, up all the way to your arms, neck and head.

Notice what feelings are birthed seemingly out of nowhere, without any knowledge of a source. But still they come rolling in, one in front, others to follow, to splash on the beach of your consciousness. They wash and clean as they break open.

All this splashing and scouring carves cathedrals of the soul, space for spirit. Inhabit the space of your spirit so that you are as big as you deserve to be.

May you enter this new day unworried by origins and excited by birthing.

Your gift today is splashing.

Allow this new day to welcome you. Early this morning I was awakened by the full moon that found an opening in the shade, and shone on my face. With the light, some heavenly touch graced my cheek to bring me out of sleep into consciousness.

That light came so many miles in silence, reflected in the stillness of space. Bring the silence of the planets down to your meditation this morning. Welcome the quiet time, precious as it is...

Even heavenly light must have somewhere to land, and perhaps reflect from. Honor your body by acknowledging its form and substance. Review your physical being as you sit here: your fingers and toes, arms and legs, torso, skull and facial features.

Close the distance between you and your emotions. Let yourself be touched by what you are feeling right now, whether it is poignancy, resentment, relief, astonishment, or a feeling that does not quite yet have a name: it is still valuable.

Even more difficult to quantify is spirit, certainly more a quality, a quality of grace, lightness, and soul. It is the quality that a distant friend calls forth when they think of you, the quality that you evoke when you think of who you really are.

May you be yourself today.

Your gift today is the moon.

Blessed be the circumstances that bring you into this day. I walk in the woods with my dog Zoey. My feet slip and slide on slick, thick ice that covers the path and flows into all the lower sections like icy lava, surrounding and freezing the tree trunks in place.

The iced flow seems to have happened eons ago, but remains in frozen silence, solid now, mute testimony to the liquid changes of yesterday. How much from the past stands preserved in silence, like ourselves. Continue your silence in these new moments...

Feel the density and presence of your physical being, mostly quite the same as it was yesterday. See anew who you are physically: your toes and feet, your legs and thighs, your waist and middle, your chest and neck, your shoulders and arms, your hands and fingers, your neck and head.

Feel what feeling might need to thaw and flow forth. Let it melt enough to move and seek out its own path, downhill, around obstacles, naturally finding its own way.

What smooths the way is spirit, the underlying steady essence of who we are. So much slips and slides during a day, during a life, but the core remains, some solid center, a destiny that is yours alone.

May you flow with the currents of this day.

Your gift today is to flow.

Heralding a new day, the light from the sun spreads slowly, as if coming up from the surface of the planet. The luminous air hovers, connecting all the different colored wood frame houses in the neighborhood and their unseen occupants.

This spreading light comes slowly, with an inexorable momentum, with the power of the revolving planet. In these moments of the earth's slow and silent revolution, find your special place…

Turn inward to your physical self and concentrate energy on your feet that hold you here, your legs that offer you mobility, your middle and chest that hold vital organs, your arms and hands that provide tools, your head and face that give you thinking and feeling senses.

Spiral down into your feelings, touch them with the magic of awareness, so they can come alive and move out toward expression, first for you and then for the universe. Whatever feeling it is, let it come up and come out.

And so your spirit, rather than be contained or distracted by emotions, is now released by the expression of feelings. There is now room, and a pathway. Enjoy this openness, use it, ride it so that your spirit is free to express.

May you turn toward the light today, whether its source is inside or outside.

Your gift today is to turn.

Welcome. In the wet woods, the close air is still sharp with the lingering cold, yet rich with earth smells. White snow and gray ice melt to reveal black and brown twigs and dirt, mixing, moving mysteriously downstream. Freshets, gurgling, appear unexpectedly in the middle of the standing trees.

While all the rest of your life moves around you, be an island of rest. Give yourself quiet at this time, this hour, this moment. Let the chaos move right on by, swirling, twirling, while you remain centered, calm, and unmoving, rooted solidly in your quiet time…

Feel what you are made of physically, your mass, form and shape. Know that you are unique. This is the only you there is: your feet and legs, your waist and torso, your chest and shoulders, your arms and hands, your head and face.

So too your emotions: even experiencing exactly the same event, none of us would have precisely the same feelings in response. As you sit here, right now, let whatever feeling arises come, be known and be expressed.

The energy of this feeling clears a pathway for spirit, scrubbing and scouring a streambed like the melting snows of winter creating new streams in the woods. Marvel at the unexpected yet powerful pathways where there is least resistance, as spirit moves in its own course.

May you find your own course today.

Your gift today is revealing.

Here is the day, and all this time stretching out in front of us, a gift that no one can duplicate. Ponderous clouds haunt the horizon, their undersides lit up brightly – yellow and orange – by light of the rising sun, itself still to appear.

Gather silence to yourself now and sit here in the quiet of these precious moments, yours alone. Bring yourself home to the shelter of your being, something only you have and only you can do, and be…

Here too is your body, your physical home that holds and nurtures your life on this planet at this time. Consider how you might take care of your body today, what you might put on it, put in it, support it, how you might love yourself in this physical way.

What is shelter but a temporary place and time where it is safe to notice and express feelings free of judgment? Let your feelings come. They arrive here where they are deeply welcomed as the truest expressions of who you are.

Then, underneath, feel your gentle spirit, or your passionate spirit. This deep core gives you your very being; without it you could not be yourself, and with it you are indeed your true self.

May you walk through this day finding resting places along the way.

Your gift today is solace.

One lone star, surprisingly bright, lingers after night to greet this sleepy, anxious earthling. The importance of earthly concerns dwindles with the darkness, and this tiniest light hangs in the sky, asks nothing, and reminds us we are here only to shine.

Beyond all the rooftops the whole huge sky silently carves out this corner of the universe for us, our home in the heavens. Now when you sit in meditation, join the silence of the stars…

Your body offers you a home in this creation. Your form is the physical expression of who you are today. No judgments. This is you: your toes and feet, your legs and knees, your middle and chest, your shoulders and arms, your hands, neck and head.

Give your attention to what feelings are shining through. They seek only to be seen. Faint or fierce, gentle or growling, the one feeling that shows up is the only one that can, so here it comes, a glistening star or a shooting star.

Shining underneath is spirit, always spirit, the one fire that never goes out. Consider how you might feed the fires of your spirit today, from both the outside and the inside.

May you be as much spirit today as body.

Your gift today is a star.

With the tentative blue morning sky in the background, the low sun keeps the far side of the old and tall trees in shadow while it paints the near side with strokes of gold. The new light demonstrates the curve and mass of the aged trunks, all the way down to their roots.

Except when wind coaxes tunes from their branches, how silent these trees stand over the years. Banish your bluster now so that the old silence can return here. For now be rooted in your own kind of stillness...

Let yourself experience this place and this connection with the earth that your body gives you. Feel your weight and mass sitting here: your trunk, your limbs, and your roots to the earth.

Shine the morning light of your awareness, the conscious act that both highlights what is near and shadows the underside. Know that all feelings are necessary, that both ecstasy and pain are part of your life.

Your inner light, like the sun, has its cycles, but remember that when your light is dim in one part of your life, it is blazing in another.

May you take care today to see both what light illuminates and what it casts into darkness.

Your gift today is to have roots.

Snow pours down. The flakes swirl and twirl in the wind, and quickly coat every surface, accumulate, pile up, and frost the world white, as if some unseen hand tips endless snowflakes from the basket of the universe high above.

All the action emphasizes the silence: how could this riotous scene happen without some noise, some rush of snowflakes pouring out of the sky, some crash as they hit the frozen ground again and again? But only white silence...

This movement is seen by an observer, sitting, breathing, a physical form. Visit your physical being now; literally remember your body, its parts, and its whole, from feet to legs, waist to chest, arms to hands, neck to head.

Consider what feelings float and crash down into your awareness, land softly or harshly on the surface of your consciousness: relief, resentment, sadness, gratitude, anxiety, hope. Each feeling is distinct from the other, just as each snowflake is uniquely different.

And even as the air seems full, there is room, space between all the flakes, as spirit pervades all the spaces in our lives, both separating and joining every act we make, every word we speak, every breath we take.

May you today feel the spaces in between.

Your gift today is pouring.

The welcoming sun carves the slanted, snow-covered rooftop into two halves, one half bright, sparkling with tiny, intense crystals of light, the other half deep, mysterious, with gray shadow, still of the night. Both halves are necessary to make a morning roof.

Still yourself so that you can notice the movement of the sun's shadow cross the earth, just as silence can move with the force of the planets across your being, right now, bringing quiet to you…

If you were sitting in the sun at this moment, your body would cast a certain unique shadow, only yours. Offer your physical being the appreciation of uniqueness, inside and out; no judgments, only love that you are who you are.

And for every feeling there is its opposite, its dark or light twin. Avoid the mixing or diluting of feelings. They stand out in contrast and gain strength from each other; each deserves its own time, its own expression.

The wider the range of emotional expression, the more room there is for spirit. Let your spirit shine through both light and shadow. Enjoy being who you are and letting your essence show.

May you find both light and dark today.

Your gift today is shadow.

Welcome to another day, yours. These days, like children playing, fiercely frost the early morning windows, and are only too glad to have the sun melt it all away in an hour.

The frost comes and goes in complete silence, its marvelous designs lost unless you pay attention, and then they are lost anyway. How quickly the lace and filigree appear and disappear. Looking inside, see the design of your life in this precious present moment…

Appreciate this body, your home for this life this day. Offer sustenance and support to your whole physical being: feet and legs, knees and thighs, waist and chest, arms and hands, neck and head.

Find that childlike place within, where you keep your carefree and frivolous self, the place of pure feelings. Not bound by reason, your feelings can simmer or explode, express how they want and need to. You are the cook.

As you look within, you enter the realm of spirit, the place of essence where your unique self lives. And when you bring yourself out to interact with the world, this is the meeting place of self and other, where you can be seen for who you are, both by yourself and by others.

May you find yourself in the presence of others today.

Your gift today is to meet yourself.

Here is a new day, stretching out in front of you like a broad river sweeping toward the sea, and with the same momentum. Carrying all before it, this river of this day accepts all the past season's runoff, changes the landscape, and deposits rich silt in new places, creating fertile soil.

Let stillness grow quickly, nourished by your body. Breathe calmly rooted in place; sit here quietly. Like the river, sweep all thought before you so that your mind is clean, and you can see all the way to your inner horizon, and beyond...

With the energy of your awareness, scan your body. Be in touch with every part of yourself and thus bring yourself together: your toes and feet, your legs and waist, your chest and ribs, your shoulders and arms, your hands and fingers, your neck, head and face.

Next inventory your feelings. Welcome what you find as signs of life. Wherever there is movement, amplify it and encourage it. Be brave enough to ride the currents of your emotions downstream, so they can join the ocean of expression.

And thus your spirit is free. Nothing holds it back. Nothing holds you back, for you are spirit. Can you give yourself this much freedom?

May you feel all the freedom that is yours today.

Your gift today is a river.

Here is another day of evolution when history continues. We share the exhilaration and the satisfaction, the outright membership in the infinite community of species this day, too.

In silence, and freed from anything that might be a restriction, such as expectation, the creative spirit flourishes again. Breathing is free and easy. Not knowing what will come in the silence of creation, anything is possible, from death to life…

What waits and creates is the body, at first, such a grounded attachment to this, our earth. What would gravity hold on to without this physical form? Your mass, your heft, your trunk, your solidity, your bones, muscle and flesh.

And feelings attach us to ourselves and to our relationships. The creative process is at work all day and all night as natural feelings are born and seek expression. Notice what feeling now flows from its source, created by you, for you, and for those around you.

Binding and bonding everything is spirit, the glue of existence. Invisible yet strong, elastic but solid, present yet ageless, spirit is both here inside me and in the far-flung universe, at the same time.

May you feel the fires of creation today.

Your gift today is evolution.

Welcome to this new day when the cavernous characters of the dream world blend with the gentle, familiar peoples of the usual day. Imagine what they would say to each other given the chance! Some would be strangers, some lovers.

They need silence for their introductions and first awkward words, shuffling like junior high kids in baggy pants. Offer this necessary silence right now, while your many characters sort themselves out. Listen to the quiet voices. Let them whisper to you. Let the silence return, as it always does…

This character you are has its own unique body, chosen by the universe for the life you are living: your feet down below, all the way to your head above.

Imagine all the feelings your many characters feel! Invite them to come on stage when they are ready and speak their parts: the anger and passion, the tenderness and mercy, the grief and solace.

Like the playwright sitting unseen in the darkened auditorium, spirit is the source of everything, forming us into a community of players. Even while you allow your own spirit to show up and speak through you, notice how it connects you to all the other players.

May you go through this day in character.

Your gift today is your character.

I step out on the front porch to join the cat, who is surveying his street. I see the chunks of remaining ice and hear the crunch of early cars breaking iced-over puddles. The cat stretches, black against the gray porch floorboards.

Then, for a few moments, there is silence, even while everything continues. Nothing stops except the noise, and in its place is stillness, moment after moment, for a surprisingly long time. The temptation is to break it before it is broken, but what if it never ended…

Stand for a few moments like a mountain: feet on the floor, legs steady and holding up the torso and trunk, and chest, with arms loose and ready to swing and wave, and then stretching up with neck and head, erect, facing forward, toward the day.

Imagine all the little nooks and crannies where feelings can hide. Search out any emotion as if you were a windstorm scouring a mountain clean, whistling into every crevice and swirling into every corner. The mountain stands clean and solid.

The mountain and the sky have spirit in common. Each creation has a unique spirit, an essence that transcends matter, space and time. Now that you are reassured about your solidity, let go enough to feel and be your spirit.

May you trust your form enough to be your spirit today.

Your gift today is a mountain.

The morning breeze brings something foreign, from another place. My dog Zoey sniffs the air. Then, in a burst of energy, she prances and dances, wanting to play. In the earth's spin there are no barriers to what the air can bring. Who knows what exotic smell could set us dancing.

Bring your dance inside to the dance halls of your mind, where you can dance as you please in the great empty silence of the ages. Let yourself feel the limitless space available inside, and do not hasten to fill it…

Sitting here, leave the silence enough to be the one who experiences the silence, and experience it with your whole physical being: your feet and legs, your thighs and waist, your middle and chest, your arms and hands, your neck and head.

So too with your emotions. If you experience a feeling, welcome it, but if not, enjoy the peace in the knowledge that sometime, maybe soon, maybe later, a feeling will show up, inevitably. It matters not what feeling it is, only that you extend your hand to it.

It is spirit that supplies the music to which we each dance our lives. Open your ears, free your feet. Feel the encouragement, the familiar tunes and the new melodies, the songs that spirit sings to you.

May you dance through this day.

Your gift today is dance.

Welcome. The fog of the night slowly melts away and the sun's warmth permeates to the inside, smooth and soothing and inviting life again, encouraging the first green shoots of spring flowers up from the still-cold earth.

The new growth happens overnight when it is most quiet. Bring similar stillness to your life right now at this moment and enjoy your inner growth as you sit in silence...

Your physical being changes and grows too, regenerating itself to continue to provide a home for you on this earth at this time. Travel inside yourself to notice these stirrings, these growings, head to toe, throughout your physical being.

Feelings break through the soil of our consciousness, seeking sunlight and rain, and room to grow. Nurture the tiniest seed, cradle it, protect it, shelter it as it grows up, blooms and flowers.

Every creation needs a spark of life, without which matter is only matter. Find again that spark of spirit, so that you know you are here, and deserve to be here among us all, with your place assured.

May you notice your newness today.

Your gift today is growth.

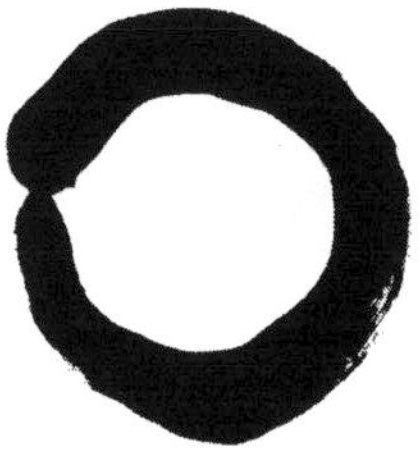

Once last night I woke from the deep dark to silver slants of moonlight. Much darkness later, the real sunlight lightens the room and brightens the room and its brilliance fills every corner.

The light, direct and reflected, requires no sound. It comes in complete silence, the better to appreciate its spiritual source and force. Let your light in and reflect it back out, here in this fullness of mind: mindfulness...

Your body sits here, quietly still, for the moment not moving. Quiet, but alive; still, but functioning. Visit each part so that you activate the whole: feet and legs, waist and chest, arms and hands, neck and head. Open your five bodily senses plus intuition.

As you tune up and tune in, experience both the shadow and the glitter of your emotions, both being necessary. Welcome the sadness, the fortitude, the despair, the bliss, the travail, and the peace: every emotion that is reflected back from the world.

Once this screen is clear, like a mirror washed clean by rain, we see enormous depths, unfathomable yet comforting. Here at last is the realm of spirit, of compassion and deep understanding. No words are needed, only the breath of life and the recognition that we are mirrors for each other.

May you see yourself in the world today.

Your gift today is reflection.

I slosh through the slush in the woods as the whole world seems loose and changing: neither ice nor water. Bean boots earn their reputation. Everything is wet, full and flowing: streams overflow their banks.

Then the gurgling and rushing waters slow and fade, and puddles form, smaller, quieter. The streams of consciousness run deep, still, creating calm surfaces of mind…

Even as this body is silent witness to all that changes on the outside, so do changes occur inside: breathing exchanges old air for new, digestion and elimination processes happen, decay and growth cycles turn and turn, and keep turning.

One emotion is felt and expressed, leaving room for another, in its turn. Transition seems sometimes like a permanent state, as feelings come and go, often in quick succession, one after another: satisfaction, sadness, fear of the unknown and elation.

Just as melting snow sluices the pathway for the runoff, so do emotions scour the way for spirit. This is a time to give in to the spirit of change and transition, to let go of a familiar form and join the flow of new creativity.

May you welcome the transformations of your day.

Your gift today is transition.

The fierce little frost does its best, working during the night to coat everything with a fine surface layer of crystal that sparkles in the morning sun. But the frost, like winter itself, fades quickly with the light of day. The gentle wind is astonishingly warm.

This time between is most welcoming of silence, as one season ends and another takes hold. Like the deeper, longer days, time stretches to include both winter and spring, and creates a fullness encompassing both seasons. Take this fullness inside and join it with your own vast stillness…

Feel the fullness of your physical being, how much it holds, how much it does, how much it is, and therefore how much you are. Send appreciation and love through your body: to your toes, feet, legs, thighs, waist, chest, shoulders, arms, hands, fingers, neck and head.

Consider the panoply of feelings you hold, your ways to respond to whatever life offers. You have a feeling for every event, every occurrence, and every circumstance. Let nothing stand in the way of having your feelings.

Largest and most encompassing of all, in fact everything, is spirit. In everything and of everything, spirit is without limit. More abundant than the sky, the earth and the sea, spirit is yours and you are spirit's.

May you stride into this day enlarged and ennobled.

Your gift today is abundance.

Welcome to a new world. The snow cover finally melts away, and reveals an expanse of ground rough with the debris of winter and raw from its ravages. Everything seems deeper, wider, longer, and higher.

While the outside world expands, let the inside world also grow larger and larger. Breath comes in and goes out. Each time your chest is a little bit more full, and each breath brings more silence inside…

Follow your breath in your nose and mouth, down your throat, into your two lungs and from there throughout your whole body: arms, hands and fingers, chest, waist, and down to your legs, feet and toes.

Stay in tune with your body and find those places that

hold emotion. Entice and encourage whatever feeling you find to grow, to grow up and out, so that the feeling is expressed right here, now.

With the way cleared by emotions, let your spirit breathe and live and come. This nameless essence is what is most uniquely you. Try on the notion that who you really are is not bound by time or space.

May you expand beyond your usual conception of yourself.

Your gift today is expansion.

Enso Morning

Welcome. Both the darkness and the snow cover have left to reveal the browns, blues, early greens and pinks of morning lawns. Not yet brilliant, the colors call invitingly, and promise new pleasures.

The colors are unearthed in the stillness of the morning. In this quiet time, this time of meditation, let them become more and more rich and vibrant, both inside and outside…

Go deep down into your body, layer by layer, and bring awareness and energy to every part of your physical being. Notice the responses you receive as your body wakes up and tingles with life: your legs and thighs, your waist and chest, your shoulders and arms, your neck and head.

Uncover your emotions so that they too emerge into awareness. Be colorful in your expressions of feelings; use a full palette to express what you feel. From bright blue, raucous red, growthful green, passionate purple, bitter black, yolky yellow, each expresses some feeling you have.

Consider what color is spirit: silver, purple, white, gold? Paint your spirit bright and shimmering; use only your own mix of colors and see them reflected in the day before you.

May you be colorful today.

Your gift today is color.

Enso Morning

Thunder rolls across the early morning sky, loud, and reminds us of gods. It welcomes the day's beginning with a rolling roar that then fades away. Even the orchestra percussionist, when she brings the drumstick down on the kettledrum, has three of her fingers poised to silence the roar.

Silence yourself now. After your own internal roaring, let there be peace and quiet, peace on earth. A peaceful moment creates another peaceful moment until there is a whole meditation…

In the stillness, feel your quiet heartbeat that sends blood coursing through your veins, and brings energy to every part of your body. Feel your physical system receiving all those nutrients and oxygen, and then releasing all the waste materials back into the air and universe.

Contact all the emotions around your body, the soft, gentle ones and the loud, harsh ones. Open the full range of feelings so they all have their due, their expression and their life. No one can offer the permission that you can.

Spirit too comes in many different forms, including when you least expect it. You may see the clouds form, but no rain falls. Sometimes drops fall from a clear sky. And occasionally a rainbow appears with no explanation, but if you are watching you will see it.

May you not fear the noise or the silence today.

Your gift today is thunder.

Welcome. The sun approaches the shore, then disappears behind thick fog, a loss of warmth and visibility. When I walk out on the rocks, the fog is so thick the only way I know I am surrounded by water is to listen to the regular swish and wet tumble of the waves breaking, unseen, but almost at my feet.

Let any noise fade into the background. As you sit here in silence, feel the refreshing quiet envelop you like a blanket, whose only function is to protect you and comfort you, and to allow you to exist inside, deep inside…

Find ways in this moment to appreciate your physical form, the body that gives you your everyday life here. Notice what parts of your physical being call out to you for special attention, and extra nurturing, and offer these healing qualities to them right now.

And do the same for your emotional self: listen with compassion to those feelings that right now ask for loving acceptance and gentle expression, or even perhaps not so gentle expression. Give yourself permission to feel what you already are feeling, and to move the feeling out into the world.

As you continue this movement, what is revealed is your essence, that fragile but eternal quality that is yours and yours alone, unique in all the world. Consider how you might honor and express your spirit.

May you appreciate the comings and goings in your life today.

Your gift today is goodbyes.

That floppy, lopsided moon leaned over with its gleaming light to break up the loud clouds, and whisked us more toward morning than we wanted to be. I sent back a message heavenward, a prayer to always be so. I acknowledge something way beyond me; I let the day come down.

And it came quietly, as it has for the centuries. We humans have, in our moments of peace and longing, sent our wishes into the universe, which has patiently listened to our prayers. Let silence reign…

The source of what radiates out is our body, our home here. Review and thus honor this physical temple of yours: the marvelous complexity of flesh and bone that allows us to breathe in and out, to give and receive.

So too do we take in and give out emotions. As our heart and gut engage, feelings arise naturally, seeking acknowledgment and expression. See what feelings live in you and long to come up and come out, and live in the world.

As the pathway is cleaned and cleared, your spirit can flow toward the ocean we all share. Practice, rather than being a body with a spirit, being a spirit with a body. In this way know no bounds, so that you can be everywhere and everyone.

Today may your intentions shine in every wish and act.

Your gift today is prayer.

Enso Morning

Welcome to a new day. The past is nowhere to be seen. This future is here, waiting, but not waiting. The sand at the beach below the tide line has no footprints but those I make fresh and new, my own path.

The waves curl softly in their fall to the sand stretched flat before them, yet the sounds are rushing and loud. Astonishingly, silence emerges, and lives in the seconds between the waves, brief and magnificent…

Sinking into the sand that receives my weight, my feet carry me across the beach. Visit each part of your body with your awareness, from your feet, up your legs and torso, to your chest, arms, hands and head, awakening.

Revisit yourself to find emotions, which need only a

brief welcome. Each one take its shape and flies through the sky of your consciousness like a shooting star, bright, its very birthing flare portending its coming demise.

Spirit is the great, unfathomable background for the busy solar systems of our lives, always there, always here, if we can but move out of the way enough to notice.

May you move enough out of the way today to notice your spirit.

Your gift today is astonishment.

From the bay islands on the left, sweeping across the sparkling morning sea to the headland on the right, the horizon stretches its welcoming arms, showing the earth's precious arc.

For so many years the silent morning sun has skipped across this sea to touch these granite shores, whether there was a human to marvel or not. Now we are here in this circle, on this silent sphere…

All in all, how small we are, yet as real and substantial as these granite rocks washed by the constant surf. And as temporary. Feel your physical self giving you presence for these moments of life: your limbs and torso, head and senses.

Flashing by in these instants, emotions come around the circle and, if not held and coveted, go. Honor not the content, but the movement: fluid and flowing, feelings birth, express, die, over and over.

Both our unique gift and our common connection, spirit is how we join the cosmos, the largest circle of all.

May you both discover and create ever-expanding circles today.

Your gift today is to be part of the circle.

The close heavens let soft raindrops fall gently to the morning earth, where they touch and wet the tender new plants. They stir up a damp smell of life and remind us how much we ourselves are made of water, and need to be watered.

The rain comes so softly it is silent. The earth opens, receives and stills itself. Be the welcoming earth: open, receiving and still…

Let your body soak up everything that nurtures you. Take in the light, the air and the sights, colors and sounds. Bring everything warm and loving in to your deepest level, through the skin down into the very bones of you.

Feel your life with every feeling you can find. In this way your feelings can nurture you and grow you. Who knows what stalwart and beautiful plant or flower will bloom here?

Whether it takes overnight or eons, the miracle of your spirit will flower. Like a plant both mysterious and familiar, or a beloved ancestor coming for a visit, your spirit calls, seeking only to flourish.

May you join this day as you would enter a flourishing garden.

Your gift this day is to bloom.

A hidden clock, set on another shore, gifts me with an earlier hour. Morning mist coaxes the earth to life and I plant four new day lilies before the rain begins.

The Buddha watches from his corner of the garden. He neither approves nor disapproves, but offers the silence of the ages…

Every physical act is life: roots finding their place in the earth, steps walking in from the garden. Feel your body move through your life, life move through your body, from head to toe.

Continue down to the less tangible emotional life, so that your feelings move through you. Bitterness or gratitude, they are all valuable, yet the same to the garden Buddha.

Your spirit inhabits the space carved out by your life. So with each breath, breathe life into your spirit.

May you have the time and space today to be planted and feel grounded.

Your gift today is roots meeting the earth.

Thanks be for a new day. The earth thanks the sky for the recent rains, holding the precious water tenderly in puddles that reflect back the still gray sky. A late drop falls into the puddle, sending ripples to the tiny shores.

Everything is in miniature, and thus without sound: one drop on the ocean of puddle, then another, still in silence. Each one starts a circle of life that ripples to the edges, and kisses the shore quietly…

Only in this physical world can we experience these truths, how one movement leads to others, how interdependent our world is. As you breathe in this morning silence, notice how your breath kisses all the shores of your body.

Touch of any kind, even from the past or future, stirs feeling in this, the present. Let your feelings stir up, stir around and overflow the shores.

This great, silent hand or breath, from without or within, is the spirit of life itself, touching and breathing you, breathing into your essence, so that you may have the life of this day.

May you be quiet enough today to feel the breath of life.

Your gift today is ripples.

The osprey lands lightly on the high, black tree branch, and settles its wide wings. Lord of the sky above and the sea below, the raptor brings fierce life to the still early morning light. The small round cove shimmers below, and receives the bird's presence.

Yet the gray morning light holds silence for now. As the pale sun climbs slowly above the tall, dark shoreline firs, the gentle stillness of night lingers on into the day…

Let your body receive everything offered at this moment, all the gifts that can be felt physically, taken in by your five senses. Absorb these gifts into your skin, your flesh and your bones: make them your own.

With no judgments, honor whatever the emotion is that lands on your awareness. Recognize the life that your feelings bring and welcome it. Every feeling is life itself, landing and seeking a home where it can have expression.

With the assurance that you can be who you really are, feel what you already feel, your spirit rejoices and surveys its kingdom spread out before it like a still bay in morning light.

This is the day for your spirit to land.

Your gift today is to receive.

The early tender blue sky, our loving womb, holds us in this new day as lovingly as a new child, which we are.

No sounds come with this embrace, only the sweet and tender silence, holding us…

Notice how your entire physical self is touched all over by this new day, and as you gratefully allow it, every single part of your body is receiving the awakening energy.

So too does the soft morning welcome and greet your emotional body. It seeks and encourages you to acknowledge and express what you already feel.

And in this first flowing of your day, the feelings – especially vulnerability – flush through, opening a path for your spirit to join all the other spirits here and there, everywhere.

May you feel in your bones your spiritual connections this day.

Your gift today is tenderness.

Enso Morning

Softly the light returns for another day. The darkness of night slowly melts away and the spaces of a new day are gently infused with enlightenment.

All this transformation comes without effort or sound. Welcome and join this new day with your own quietude…

Let this day's light, as energy, spread throughout your entire physical being – from head to toe – awakening and energizing as it goes.

Because we are human, we feel. Trust and honor – which means express appropriately – whatever it is that you are already feeling today: affection, nostalgia, annoyance, appreciation, etc.

And in so doing, and being, you find your spirit, and your spirit finds you. Enjoy the reunion and express who you are as spirit.

May your spirit join the spirit of this day.

Your gift today is to join.

The planet turns effortlessly into this new day, offering everything to you, yet again. With the light of the day – only eight minutes from the sun – comes possibility.

The new dawn comes with gentle ease, and a silent hum of energy – the quiet vibration of life itself. Hear and feel the silence spread inside and out…

A slight increase of energy will set your cells dancing, will tune your organs, will energize your body systems, and wake you up.

More subtle, but no less important, emotions wake up too, simply seeking expression: gratitude, relief, anger, sadness, love – whatever its name the emotion expresses who you are – to yourself and to others.

Similarly, your spirit has multiple forms, all of them longing for the chance to manifest in the world.

May your spirit multiply and flourish today.

Your gift today is ease.

As this day begins, both the darkness that leaves and the lightness that arrives occupy all the space.

Stretch out into the silent space between things all around you, and add your silence to the emptiness that is not empty...

Experience your body taking up space: expand fully into the outer edges of your physical self. Stretch to your full circumference.

Expand your emotional being so that you allow feelings to fill you up on their way to outward expression. Know that you always have room for new feelings.

As the way is thus prepared, live your spirit. Be who you are, ageless, spacious, precious, unique: your own spiritual person.

May your being fill you to your boundaries and beyond this day.

Your gift today is space.

With the morning's first light comes the astonishing trumpet-like array of peeps, calls and chirps of a mockingbird, demanding attention to a new day.

Then, inexplicably, silence spreads out into the whole world, and covers every corner like a soft blanket, bringing deep peace...

Let this calm actively inhabit every part of your physical being, so that you pulse with energy as your body awakens, head to toe.

To awaken your cells brings life to your feelings. Emotional juices flow like a fresh stream bubbling through a field and overflowing its banks.

Spirit flows now, through these scoured pathways, spilling out over the landscape of your life and beyond.

Today may there be no bounds to the expression of your spirit.

Your gift today is boundlessness.

Welcome. The greened Buddha sits at home in the corner of our small yard, with tall, new, red tulips behind him, peaceful, eyes closed yet seeing everything. My two-year-old neighbor asks, "Why are his eyes closed?"

Let this present moment be silent, unstructured by distraction, and open to awareness...

Find your physical flesh and bones, and come back home again, to this human being you inhabit. Make yourself at home in your body.

Feelings also need a place to be welcomed, safely shared, and thereby make their way out into the larger world: relief, anger, peace, sadness, wonder, awe, etc.

So too do spirits and souls seek a familiar home where they may be embraced: your spirit wants you.

May your full self be at home in the world this day.

Your gift today is home.

Welcome. What is this new day but a sequence of opportunities to see the world through your own eyes, a reflection of who you are.

In this early moment, let your mind find some silence like the still surface of a small rain puddle or a vast lake. Knowing they are all the same…

Expand this awareness, touching with the energy of your mind your toes, feet, legs, middle, chest, arms, neck and head.

These are the living places of your feelings, which seek motion and release, awareness and expression.

Your spirit follows the twin encouragements: deepen

and expand. Both inside and outside, reflect your spirit.

May you shine and share your enlightenment with the world today.

Your gift today is to reflect.

Just as the day welcomes you – all qualities of you – you can welcome the day knowing it will bring a variety of experiences. Welcome or not, here is the day.

Even the silence has a texture, now rough, now smooth, now thin, now full. As the quiet unfolds, simply be aware of its changes…

Your body breathes and pulsates its way into the day given to life. Blood is pumped and circulates, muscles contract and expand, breath comes in and goes out.

The landscape of emotions has peaks and valleys, gentle rolling hills and high, craggy peaks, and all the weather in between. Inhabit this enlivening land, which may have a tempest or a lull.

Your spirit, who you have always been, and always will be, is woven together of threads coarse and fine, old and new, bright and dark, noisy and quiet.

May you embrace the thunder and the peace of this day.

Your gift today is the storm before the calm.

The spreading light of this new day washes away the night's darkness; the old melts away, the new emerges.

Silence covers your earth home and holds you in its hearth, that word so close to heart. Your world is quiet…

Surface skin is cleansed. Let the fresh scouring of the new day all the way in, down to your bone marrow.

The emptiness of your being awaits what you truly feel. Your emotions can and will bubble up to the surface, looking for air and space to be free.

Spirit pervades and invades all and everything, the essence of purity and of transcendence: your familiar spirit.

May you be your spirit starting anew every moment this day.

Your gift today is cleanliness.

The shimmering golden hand of morning sunlight warms the wall with light that just came 100 million miles to me, and to you.

This light burns all that way quietly, bringing its fiery announcement in absolute silence…

Softly let your physical being warm up; let each part awaken as you sense, stretch, contract, expand, and move, head to toe.

And the fragile flame of feeling is finally recognized for what it is: the birth of emotion, the heat of life.

Similarly, the spark of your soul flickers, grows warmer and radiates out into the world. You are another sun.

May you warm yourself with the universe's energy today.

Your gift today is heat.

The day opens before you as an untrodden path. Only you can walk yourself through this day of days.

Silence is everywhere, underneath everything. It is like deep bedrock that is available whenever we touch it. Now let your mind walk in silence...

All we have is our physical body, our home while we are here on the earth. With your mind and your body, touch every part, inner and outer, that you are.

Inside and outside, our emotions are numerous, and complex; they have lives of their own. Feelings cry out for acknowledgement of their existence, and expression.

Be inspired – inspirited – by what you feel. In this way spirit is found and encouraged. Today let your spirit venture forth.

May you meet yourself on your walk through this day.

Your gift today is to walk.

After a night of darkness, welcome to the dawn of a new cosmos. But when did you ever leave? There is nowhere to go but be here, now in the eternal present.

Imagine the immensity of the silence of the ages, pouring endlessly over all existence, holding all creation – you – in its long loving embrace…

We know now that despite all of physical matter, and its distractions, most of our universe is empty space. Honor and nurture your rare and precious physical being.

Rare too, our emotions exist to remind us that we alone – and together – are human, uniquely possessed of the extraordinary ability to cry, laugh, love, rage, smile, and weep at all of our life's teachings.

Where we join the entire cosmos is with our spirit. Across space and through time we are so valuable as to be one with everything.

May you lose your sense of time today.

Your gift today is eternity.

At this first slim early light, the day is only this: a sweet and gentle small misted miracle of morning for you to enjoy.

Such stillness reigns, this great quiet that existed before all the noise and will exist afterwards. Meditate on eternity...

After awakening in your house, your temple, your physical home while you walk this earth this time, bring the energy of your five senses to enliven your body. Wake up your physical self.

Now give attention to your emotional being, the scared, rambunctious or blissful little one inside who experiences every feeling fiber of life.

This radiant attention opens your soul, both root and branch of your being, readying you for both inward and outward flight.

May you bring the peace of meditation into your day.

Your gift today is meditation.

Out of the dark night emerges the great fan of high tree branches that reach for the sky and encourage the day to lighten, so they can be seen.

This longing for the light continues without sound, without movement, and needs only breath and awareness...

Solid, planted here like a great tree, your body is rooted in mother earth, yet moves freely, waking to the day.

Feelings also move, one after the other, always new because there is no formula for life's feelings. Welcome your spontaneous feelings into existence, which is what they long for.

Under everything, over everything, is your soul, timeless, placeless, patient unless ignored, always true, always you.

May you allow yourself to long for your best life.

Your gift today is longing.

This new day in the far high sky, clouds speak and tell me about the presence and power of unseen winds. What drives the winds drives us all.

No sounds come between my human gaze and that high sky. Only quiet fills the distance and unites us with the planets and whatever lies beyond...

We stand here on this earth planet, place of the pain and pleasure our bodies know so well. Live in your physical home now. Fill all your rooms with the sensations of life, head to toe.

Full of these fine feelings brimming is your self. Feel what you already feel, and then let the winds carry it up and away.

Cleaned and cleared out, what remains is soul essence, that which you always have been and always will be, today and forever.

Today may you feel your connection with unseen forces.

Your gift today is the sky.

As the dark of night gives way to this new day a child would ask, "Where does the darkness go?" We can live the question without an answer.

This silent mystery unfolds anew, for us, in this peaceful here and now, time and place...

This pulsating, breathing body is host to us, giving us life. Bring awakening to the parts that make up the whole: your feet, legs, middle, chest, arms, hands, neck and head.

Also parts and whole is your emotional body, keeper and expresser of a full range of energy-giving feelings.

And what of your soul this day? This essence of yours

seeks to be nurtured and seeks to be expressed.

May you experience this day with child-like wonder.

Your gift today is the here and now.

The blessings of another day are here. Without knowing exactly what form they will take, we open our deepest selves to the endless shower of possibilities.

Let this stream of creation surround you with silence. Accept the offered peace and tranquility of these moments of silence...

Become aware of your flesh and bones and all they hold, the wondrous organs that sustain your life. Your skin, that frontier where you and the world meet, that holds you together and welcomes you home.

Every single feeling noticed, alert and expressed, adds to your being who you are and how you share your divinity with the world.

The shared spark of your soul soars forth in flight, across the room, across space, across time, and transcends all and everything.

May you loosen your boundaries today.

Your gift today is divinity.

The light of the new day comes out of the night. It comes around naturally in the cycle of dark and light, and with it this new day emerges from a period of rest to a time of activity.

Launch into this time in and of silence, for when all the distractions disappear, stillness is uncovered…

Notice who it is that is sitting here in your body: you in physical form, every cell making up such an exquisite whole body, head to toe.

In the great cycle, countless repetitions of feelings come and go, come and go: rest and activity. Emotions move, pulse, expand, contract, express. Then they rest.

Who you are as spirit likewise rests, then breathes your soul out to the world, out into the universe.

Today may you both rest yourself and express yourself.

Your gift today is rest.

The great light of the sun makes its way into the sky hours before the actual ball of fire appears over the horizon. The sun's light touches everything that is not closed off from it. It gives both penetrating light and obscuring shadow.

All this happens in its own time and in silence. The few minutes it takes the sun's energy to leave there and arrive here are silent minutes; despite the vast distance and the enormous speed it is a silent journey…

The sun warms your entire body, head to toe. Feel the sun's energy land onto your skin and pour into your bloodstream.

Heat stirs emotions, so let your feelings warm up,

move and express.

Your spirit is beyond warmth and cold, and is bound by neither time nor space.

Whether you see it or simply feel it, may you bask and bathe in the warm energy of the sun today.

Your gift today is the sun.

The open lawn with its short but still-green grass beckons, sloping gently down to the harbor water, an easy early morning walk. Let these first moments of the day be as easy as a stroll downhill to the beach.

Find a resting place where your feet can stop and your mind can rest. You become the still point. Everything else is exposed for the distraction it is. You keep returning to the silence, new each time…

Feel your physical body, compact at first, now stretching as you inhale and exhale. Breathe into your limbs, and your middle, and lastly your neck and head. As you provide energy your body comes alive.

Drop down into your emotional life at this moment.

What feeling do you find? No judgment necessary, only acknowledgment of what is ready to express. Take heart, for you have found your heart that seeks expression.

Take heart, too, for you have begun to touch your soul. When the distractions are gone, as happens in time of crisis, the path down to the soul lies open, downhill to the beach and ocean. Find yourself at the shore of your soul, and have courage to stay there for a while.

May you unfold, as if you were getting up and walking down to the ocean. Let your step be both sure and easy.

Your gift today is unfolding.

Recognize that you exist today. The most basic and precious fact.
Along with all of creation, you are alive still and again.

Most of creation is silent, the quiet underneath the noise. Join the immense background that holds us all, the great stillness underneath everything. Be silence now…

This form you have is like no other, but uniquely your physical manifestation for this human life. It asks for honor and care in every present moment.

We have the gift of feeling, our natural responses to being alive. Our feelings remind us that we are here and that we are awake and responsive.

Your spirit is alive and well. Your spirit infuses your life with energy and meaning; it is the constant amidst all the change.

May you know the simple gift of being here and now.

Your gift is existence.

Open your eyes to a new day. Awaken to the unknown, for the known has not happened yet. Be in this moment, the brand new moment, just born.

Bring this awakened self into the precious stillness of your conscious being. Sit here in stillness that weaves all the moments together…

Bring awareness to your form, this body. When you notice, you offer energy, as you do now, to your physical being in this time, in this place. Your body is one with all other forms.

Be aware now of your emotional life in this moment, what you feel. Honor each and every feeling as they come and go; express one at a time.

Animating all this is spirit. We are not so much conscious of each form, but consciousness itself, together, the world of spirit.

May you be awake and alive to your day today.

Your gift today is consciousness.

Welcome. When I am living on a boat I love to get up early, raise the sails in the calm morning stillness, slip the mooring, and head out of the harbor. Often the wind is so gentle it makes no mark on the water but propels the boat. Let the day propel you.

Continue this beginning in silence. The wind, silent, is joyful. Be like silent wind. Fill yourself with silence, bringing calm to every cell…

Flesh out the form you are. Give attention and energy to your feet up through your legs and middle to your chest and arms, and finally to your neck and head. Honor, awaken and energize yourself to this day.

Call up your emotions. Roam your consciousness for a

feeling. It matters not which feeling comes. What gives life and health is the process, so that whatever feeling arises is welcomed.

Given the opportunity of this new day, how might your soul be acknowledged today? Here and now we have the courage to call forth your precious soul. What or who answers the call?

May you sail into this day and create ways to express who you are. Any creative act may do this, any way through which you can touch, speak, see and express your bliss.

Your gift today is bliss.

Afterword

Now that you have read some or all of these Morning Blessing Letters that I wrote addressed to you, it is time for you to write your own letters to yourself, or at least give yourself similar blessings every morning, and throughout your day. To the extent that you have resonated and responded to these letters, you know what you long for, you know what you need every morning. Only you can write further letters. Now you know yourself. You know how to welcome yourself to each day. You know how to find, create, and encourage silence, and how to use the silence for meditation. You know how to honor and nurture your physical being. You know how to access and express your feelings. You know how to bring forth your spirit. You know how to offer yourself an appropriate blessing. And you know that you can offer yourself a unique gift. Finally, now you know to live as a whole spiritual being.

Biography

Rev. Jacob Watson, D. Min., is an interfaith minister, and the founding Abbot of the Chaplaincy Institute of Maine, an interfaith wisdom school. Following years as a grief counselor and hospice chaplain, he devotes his life to teaching, writing and meditation.

Contact Information
Jacob Watson
(207) 761-2522
jacobw@gwi.net
www.revjacobwatson.com

A portion of the proceeds from sales of this book will benefit the education and service work of the non-profit Chaplaincy Institute of Maine:

Chaplaincy Institute of Maine
Post Office Box 3833
Portland, Maine 04104
(207) 347-6740
www.chimeofmaine.org

Zen Enso Circles

Black Enso circles are available as note cards, prints and hanging banners. Colored Enso circles are available as prints. They are especially useful for providing a graceful focus point for meditation spaces.